Discovering
DERBYSHIRE AND THE PEAK DISTRICT

Joan P. Alcock

Shire Publications Ltd.

CONTENTS

INTRODUCTION

It is perhaps surprising that Derbyshire, which is noted for its scenic beauty, should so often have led England in industrial technology. The Romans extracted the lead, the eighteenth-century mill-owners took advantage of water power and modern industry ruthlessly exploits the natural resources of coal, limestone and gritstone. Eastern Derbyshire is heavily industrialised and in the western areas the boundaries of the National Park swing inward to avoid the industrial scene. South Derbyshire is intensively cultivated — a market-gardening area lying in the flood plain of the Trent.

In spite of this Derbyshire has much to delight the eye. It has at least five of the finest country houses in Britain, and numerous smaller houses fit into the landscape as part of the English architectural tradition. The wide variety of scenery, most of it unspoilt, was the main reason why the Peak District National Park was founded in December 1950 and this year (1972) it celebrates its 21st year. The park covers 542 square miles and though the bulk of it is in Derbyshire it includes part of Cheshire and Staffordshire. The outstanding beauty of the landscape from Dovedale in the south to Kinder Scout in the north is enhanced by its geological and biological content and the rich cultural heritage.

A Calendar of Events in the National Park is available from March onwards each year. It includes the dates of the well dressings, gardens open to the public, fairs, and much else of interest. Send a stamped addressed envelope to National Park Office, Aldern House, Baslow Road, Bakewell, Derbyshire, DE4 1AE.

I am indebted to several organisations and individuals for their help in providing information and to my mother for her help as companion on the journeys.

Well dressing

Well dressing is almost entirely confined to Derbyshire. Even here, only certain villages attempt this intricate art and enthusiasm for it rises or wanes according to local support. Wells have been venerated from antiquity but well dressing as such seems to have become established in the eighteenth century, although Tissington claims an earlier date.

Wells are dressed with pictures made from flower petals, seeds, cones, grasses and such like (plate 6). Clay is kneaded to the right consistency and pressed into trays about an inch deep, keyed to hold the clay in place when they are placed upright. The surface is smoothed, a pattern of the picture — usually a biblical scene — is placed on it, and the outline pricked out. Seeds are put along the outlines which are then filled in, firstly those requiring moss or bark, lastly those requiring flower petals. This is a skilled task requiring great patience. The petals are arranged in rows from the bottom upwards, each overlapping the next and fixed into position by the pressure of a finger or a sharp pointed instrument. It must be a co-operative effort, for the eyestrain would be too much for one person.

The most difficult parts are facial expressions, especially the eyes. Artificial flowers can be used but the best pictures are those made entirely from living plants. Barlow uses whole flowers with the stalks pushed into the clay. Tissington, the first of the well dressings, makes use of spring flowers; Eyam, in the autumn, uses berries, mosses and seeds. The pictures are at their best for the first three days. After that they begin to crack, especially in a dry spell. A good picture is a considerable achievement and one hopes that this Derbyshire custom will continue to give pleasure and excite admiration.

The actual dates of well dressing vary each year but the approximate times are as follows: Tissington, Ascension Day; Wirksworth and Endon (Staffordshire), late May; Ashford, Trinity Sunday; Youlgreave and Litton, near St. John the Baptist's day; Tideswell and Hope, late June or early July; Bakewell and Buxton, mid July; Bonsall and Stoney Middleton, late July or early August; Bradwell, early August; Barlow, the Wednesday after the second Saturday in August; Wormhill and Eyam, late August or early September.

ROUTE 1

SHEFFIELD — Curbar — Baslow — Edensor — Chatsworth — Beeley — Rowsley — Stanton-in-Peak — Birchover — Parwich — Alsop-en-le-Dale — Tissington — Thorpe — Dovedale — Ilam — Hope — Alstonefield — Hartington — Monyash — Ashford-in-the-Water — Little Longstone — Great Longstone — Hassop — Grindleford — SHEFFIELD (70 miles).

Leave **Sheffield** by A621 for Bakewell passing Abbeydale Industrial Hamlet, a late eighteenth-century steel and scythe works now containing industrial displays. The road climbs up to Ramsley Moor, the eastern edge of the Pennines, open country of heather and moss. When the road drops look for the crossroads and turn right for Curbar along a road giving a view across Eyam Moor and dropping steeply to gritstone **Curbar.** Wellington's monument to the left, marks the end of Baslow Edge. Go through the village and turn left at A623 for Baslow. **Calver** mill, six storeys high, with pedimented frontage, was built as a cotton mill about 1785. **Baslow** is entered at Bridge End, the original nucleus of the village, centred round St. Anne's church. The old bridge has a small toll-house on it (plate 1). Pass the church and turn right for Buxton (A619). Cross the newer bridge over the river which flows through Chatsworth Park, and continue along B6012 for Chatsworth.

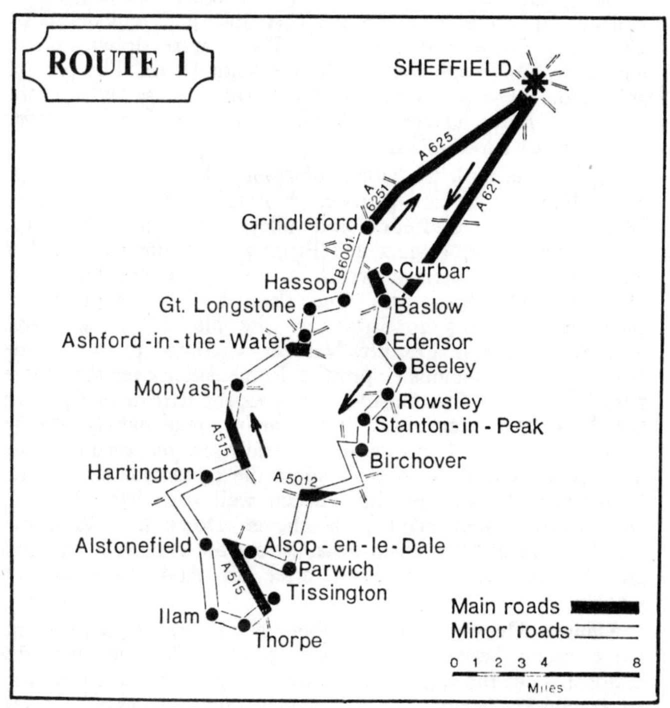

Edensor, at the entrance to the park, is a model estate village of 1839-40. Originally an older village stood within sight of Chatsworth House but the sixth Duke of Devonshire ordered the cottages to be demolished. His gardener, Joseph Paxton (of Crystal Palace fame), planned a new village and John Robertson designed the houses in a variety of styles from Norman to Swiss chalet.

Go through the park. **Chatsworth House** (open to the public) (plates 2 and 3) is one of the great houses of England, with splendid rooms full of art treasures. William Talman began the replacement of the Elizabethan house in 1687 and Thomas Archer completed the bowed north wing and the dignified west front. Court artists Louis Laguerre and Antonio Verrio painted the walls, Samuel Watson of Heanor carved in wood so perfectly that the work was long thought to be by Grinling Gibbons, Tijou cast in iron. The gardens, laid out in formal array for the first duke and remodelled by Capability Brown for the fourth Duke, were drawn into a whole by Sir Joseph Paxton for the sixth Duke. The present splendour of Chatsworth replaces that house where the unhappy Mary, Queen of Scots, yearned for freedom under the guard of Sir William Cavendish.

Beyond the park the village of **Beeley** shows the same type of architecture as at Edensor. A road leads up to Beeley Moor, giving views of edges and valleys. Keep on for **Rowsley.** At A6 turn right (signposted Buxton) opposite the shell of Rowsley railway station which served the ducal houses at Haddon and Chatsworth. The Peacock Inn was a house built in 1652 by John Stevenson who placed his name and date over the door. Dorothy Vernon is reputed to have come here during her famous elopement. Immediately over the bridge turn left towards Stanton-in-Peak, cross the narrow bridge over the Wye and bear right. The narrow road winds steeply upwards towards Stanton Moor; below, in the distance, the Wye twists and turns. Go ahead at the crossroads and at the T junction facing the high church wall turn left, climbing the hill, then keep right to Birchover. Down the hill is the small village of **Stanton-in-Peak.** Below the church is the inn, the Flying Childers, named after an Arab racehorse of Charles II.

Stanton Moor is a plateau about a mile square, a gritstone ridge rising between the valleys of the Derwent and the Bradford. On the edge of the plateau, where the road descends to Birchover, is one of the few gritstone quarries still being worked. Nearby are some notable Bronze Age remains — several barrows, Nine Ladies' Stone Circle and the monolithic King's Stone.

Birchover's houses are built of gritstone. At the foot of the hill are Rowtor Rocks in which Thomas Eyre cut seats for himself and his friends — an eighteenth-century conceit. He built the church (altered in the nineteenth century) as an act of reparation for dabbling in black magic. In the porch is a plaque commemorating Joan Waster, who was burned at the stake in Derby during the Marian persecution. Go through the village, turn left (B5056) for Ashbourne and in two miles turn right (signposted to Newhaven and Elton).

Follow the straight track between the walls for two miles and at A5012 turn right. (The route can be shortened by following A5012 and turning right at A515. After two miles take a road on the right leading to Monyash, where the route can be rejoined.) To see the Dovedale area, after joining A5012 take the first turn left (signposted Parwich). The high Minninglow embankment on the left supported the Cromford and High Peak Railway line, built by Josiah Jessop and opened in the 1830s. This is now the High Peak Trail, open to walkers and with access points for cars at Friden, Black Rocks picnic site, near to Cromford, and Middleton Top Engine House, near to Wirksworth. The Engine House is open on Sundays.

After crossing the track, keep left, go straight on at the small crossroads and after a mile keep left at the junction. The road begins to drop revealing Parwich in the valley. Turn right at the next junction signposted Parwich and Buxton. **Parwich** is a small village with a Victorian church; the Norman tympanum and font are of interest. Turn sharp left after the village green and follow the signs to **Alsop-en-le-Dale** whose small church, lying opposite the seventeenth-century hall, has a Norman nave. At A515 turn left. The Alsop car park may be used by those walking the Tissington Trail. After two miles turn left again for **Tissington**, a delightful village whose well dressing on Ascension Day is the first of the year. This village has five wells, each visited in procession from the church. The Fitzherberts have cared for the village for 400 years, occupying the seventeenth-century hall opposite Hall Well (plate 4). Their tombs are in the church, a basically Norman structure, renovated in 1854. Inside notice the two-decker pulpit, the royal arms of George I and the Norman tub-font. The churchyard looks down on the village street and the school (1837) close by the pond. Take the road opposite the church, lined with limes, go through the gate and cross A515 for Thorpe and Dovedale. At the Dog and Partridge, turn right, then left. The road passes Peveril of the Peak Hotel, swings into **Thorpe** village, then descends towards **Dovedale** (see page 62).

At **Ilam** village bear right at the Memorial Cross, and right again up the hill to Alstonefield. (A road to the left leads to the Manifold valley.) After two miles a sharp right turn leads to **Hope** village, from where the road rises to **Alstonefield.** Take the left fork for Hartington and after two miles bear right and keep on to the give-way sign. Turn right (B5054) for Hartington. Previous to this our route has passed a road leading to **Beresford Dale,** accessible on foot either from here or from Hartington. Charles Cotton lived at Beresford Hall and was host to Isaac Walton whose *Compleat Angler,* first published in 1653, is the fisherman's bible. One hotel in **Hartington** commemorates Cotton but the hall is in ruins. Built in 1611 Hartington Hall is now a youth hostel. The medieval church has some fine gargoyles.

As we climb out of Hartington through Hand Dale we again reach stone-wall country. At the give-way sign turn left (A515) and take the next right turn towards Monyash. A road to the right leads to the Bronze Age circle of **Arbor Low,** overlooked by Gib Hill, a large tumulus. Keep on for Monyash and in the village turn right for Bakewell. **Monyash** (the name means 'many ash trees') was a lead-mining centre with the right to hold a market. It still holds one twice yearly at Whitsun and on August Bank Holiday, round the market cross on the village green. St. Leonard's church is fourteenth century with a twelfth-century doorway and tower.

Just beyond the village is the beginning of the footpath through **Lathkill Dale,** with trout and grayling lurking in its stream. Keep on towards Bakewell and in 2½ miles take an awkward left turn towards Sheldon. The view to the left shows the extent of the stone-wall country. Turn right through Kirkdale descending steeply to Ashford. At A6 turn right and take the next left (B6465) into **Ashford-in-the-Water,** a pretty village with two bridges, one dating to 1664 and the other, Sheepwash Bridge, retaining the enclosure used for dipping sheep. The church was rebuilt in 1870 but has a Jacobean pulpit and four funeral garlands or crants, which were carried before a maiden's coffin and hung in the church afterwards. It was round this area that the 'black marble' was quarried which is often seen in Derbyshire church furnishings.

Turn right (B6465) for Wardlow and Monsal Head and at **Little Longstone** pull up by the hotel for the fine view of **Monsal Dale**. The Wye flows down Upper Dale under the railway viaduct and curves round the foot of Putwell Hill. Take the right turn to **Great Longstone** which is set round a tiny green covered with daffodils in spring, overlooked by the Crispin Inn. The ball-topped gateway leads to the Georgian Hall. The church was restored by Norman Shaw in 1873 and contains the Eyre pew. The Eyres lived at Hassop Hall and in the centre of the village we turn left for **Hassop.** Stone walls give place to hedges and the route runs beside the walls surrounding the Hall. It ends at the Roman Catholic All Saints built in 1814 in classical style by Joseph Ireland. Turn left (B6001), pass the Eyre Arms and descend towards Calver. At the traffic lights continue along B6001 which becomes A6521 at **Grindleford,** a small village developed as a commuter area for Sheffield after the opening of the Manchester-Sheffield railway in 1894. The road climbs through Padley Woods, protected natural oak woods. Turn right along A625 then left by the **Fox House Inn,** believed to be Whitcross where Charlotte Bronte wrote that Jane Eyre descended from the coach 'absolutely destitute' of money and hope and slept the night under a 'moss-blackened granite crag'. The road passes Houndkirk Moor and soon tall blocks of flats appear on Sheffield's skyline.

ROUTE 2

SHEFFIELD — Hathersage — Hope — Edale — Castleton — Bradwell — Peak Forest — Peak Dale — Buxton — Chelmorton — Miller's Dale — Tideswell — Foolow — Eyam — Grindleford — Abney — SHEFFIELD (70 miles).

Leave **Sheffield** on A625 and just before Ecclesall church turn right along Ringinglow Road for **Ringinglow.** At the give-way keep right, pass the Hammer and Pincers and keep straight on at the crossroads, where the curiously designed octagonal toll-house faces the equally curious architecture of the Norfolk Arms. Beyond here the National Park is entered and the moors stretch out, much of Hallam Moor on the right being the remains of peat bog. From the bridge there is a view down Burbage Brook to the valley of the Derwent. At the fork keep left. (The right fork leads to

Stanage Edge, an outcrop of Kinderscout grit, and character-istic of the 'edges' of north Derbyshire, steeply dropping on one side and sloping on the other. The stone used to be quarried for building and for millstones. Groups of the latter, roughly hewn out, can be seen abandoned along the edge. Millstones have been set up on the roadsides to mark the entrances to the Park.) The road begins to descend. To the left is **Carl Wark**, a Dark Age fort set on a small plateau, and Millstone Edge, whose name recalls its former industrial use.

At the give-way turn right (A625) which drops to Hathers-age giving a view across the Derwent Valley to Eyam Moor. **Hathersage** lies on the valley slopes. The church is fourteenth-century with fifteenth-century additions. The east window came from Derwent church and was put in when Derwent village was submerged in 1949 by the Ladybower Reservoir. In the churchyard is the reputed grave of Little John who is said to have returned to his birthplace after burying Robin Hood at Kirklees Priory (plate 7). Charlotte Bronte stayed nearby with Ellen Nussey and Hathersage is recognisable as the 'Morton' of *Jane Eyre*. Possibly she took the name of her heroine from the family whose brasses are in the church.

Continue along A625 to **Hope** (plate 6). The route can turn left at the Traveller's Rest for Tideswell but to see Edale, sited at the beginning of the Pennine Way turn right (Edale Road) opposite the medieval church. The road winds along the valley of the Noe with Blackden Edge rising in the distance. This is gritstone country. There are only two entrances to **Edale** and for centuries the people were a closely knit community holding aloof from the rest of the Peak. The coming of the railway and the popularity which the valley has for walkers have changed this. Just before Edale a long three-storey building is an old lace-thread spinning mill of 1795. Mill girls walked over the fells from Castleton to work in it.

The village of Edale clustered round the Nag's Head, lies at the foot of the Pennine Way which begins its climb up to Kinder Scout. On the opposite side of the valley is Mam Tor. Continue along the valley road for Chapel-en-le-Frith. After a narrow bridge the road winds upwards giving a splendid view over the valley. At the junction with A625 on Rushup Edge turn left for Castleton. The road winds past the foot of **Mam Tor**, the shimmering mountain, 1696 feet high and one of the seven wonders of the Peak. It is composed of shale and its east face is constantly being eroded. It can be climbed and there is an Iron Age fort on the top. On the descent to **Castleton** we pass Peak Cavern (60 feet high) and the Blue John Mines, famous for topaz- coloured spar-stone. Speedwell Cavern is on Winnat's Pass. The caverns are partly natural, the result of water on limestone, and partly man-made in the search for lead. Now they are a tourist attraction. **Peveril Castle** (plate 9) high on the crag, hovers over the gritstone houses crowded in the square. It was originally built by William Peveril, one of the Conqueror's followers, but the keep dates from 1176. **Cave Dale,** below the castle, which can be reached from the village square, climbs up to the moor. The church, restored in the nineteenth century, has eighteenth-century box-pews. One old custom survives. On Garland Day (29th May) a horseman representing Charles II rides through the village wearing a bell-shaped garland (plate 8). After the procession the garland is hoisted to the top of the church tower.

Go along A625 to Hope and one mile beyond, turn right (B6049) for Tideswell via **Brough** which takes its name from the old English *burgh* — a fort. The fort is Roman and its remains are to the west. Nearby is evidence of Derbyshire

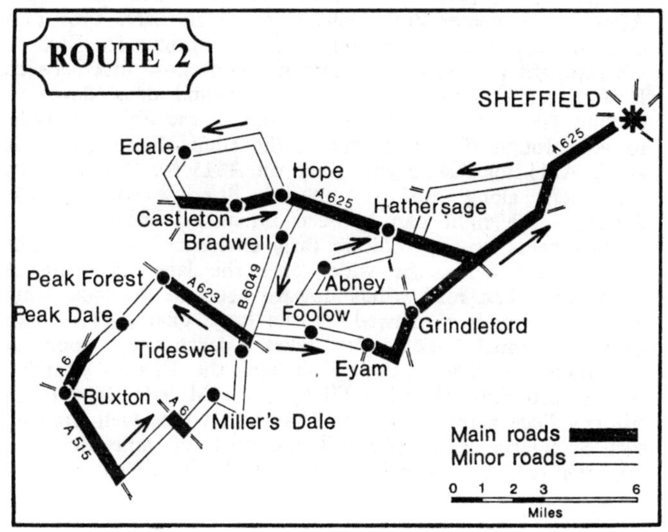

industry — the extraction of shale for cement workings. Keep on through **Bradwell** and Bradwell Dale, cut through the limestone. From Bradwell a Roman road leads across the uplands to Peak Forest. At the end of the Dale is Hazlebadge Hall (dating from 1549) part of the dowry which Dorothy Vernon brought to Sir John Manners. **Little Hucklow** is to the right and **Great Hucklow** to the left in the shadows of Hucklow Edge from which gliders soar. The route can be shortened by taking a left turn and rejoining it at Eyam (page 13). When B6049 meets A623 turn right (signposted Stockport) and in just over three miles reach **Peak Forest.**

The church at Peak Forest is one of the few in the country dedicated to King Charles the Martyr. One window shows the king in armour with an axe and block by his side; the other recalls a more recent tragedy, the murder of Lord Frederick Cavendish. The nineteenth-century church replaces an earlier chapel, founded by Christian, Countess of Devonshire, in 1657. In the eighteenth century it became the Derbyshire Gretna Green when ministers issued marriage licences to all eloping couples. The 1757 Marriage Act failed to check this happy state of affairs which continued until 1804.

Turn left at Peak Forest for Peak Dale, then bear right. After a mile comes **Peak Dale**, scene of intensive extraction of limestone, white, dusty and ruthless. Continue for Buxton. The straight road is due to Roman planning—a link between Brough and Buxton. At A6 turn left and drop down to **Buxton** (see page 59). At the bottom of the hill turn right to go through the town and at the traffic lights turn left along A515 for Ashbourne. Keep on A515 for 3 miles then turn left along A5270 opposite Brierlow Bar garage. Away to the right can be seen intensified enclosure. The narrow fields usually indicate early enclosure along the line of the strip fields, the wider ones the later enclosure of open land. The road winds upward soon to overlook King Sterndale, which is marred by the huge quarry. The edge of the National Park in fact takes a large sweep south at this point to exclude Peak Dale and the Buxton quarries. At A6 turn right, then left (B6049) for Miller's Dale. From **Miller's Dale** a road leads to **Wormhill,** whose well dressing each September decorates a well in memory of James Brindley, the canal engineer, born in 1716 at nearby Tunstead.

Go through **Tideswell** (see page 66), cross A623 and continue along B6049. Take the first right turn and at the give-way, turn right for Foolow and Eyam. At **Foolow** chapel, inn, hall and manor stand round a small green with a pond and a cross. Continue for Eyam. On the left rises Eyam Edge, riddled with ancient lead mines. Black Hole Mine is still being worked—now for fluorspar. Derbyshire is famous for its lead. The Romans mined it as early as A.D. 117 and the medieval kings gained a royalty for the ore, even exporting it. Demand was great for roofing material and drainage pipes. A code of laws grew up, based on the local customs, which were (and are) administered by the Barmote Court sitting at Wirksworth (see page 67).

Eyam has a lovely seventeenth-century hall. Opposite are the stocks on the tiny green. The church is basically of the thirteenth century but much restored and altered (plate 11). In the churchyard is a Saxon cross (plate 17) and the tomb of Catherine Mompesson, wife of William Mompesson, rector in that terrible year in Eyam's history, 1665-66. Mompesson closed the village to the world after the arrival of a box of infected clothing but five-sixths of the village died from the plague. The cottages display lists of the persons who died in them and on the hillside are the Riley graves, where lie seven members of the Hancock family, and Mompesson's well, where money was left in payment for food brought by outsiders. The pulpit from which Mompesson preached is in the church but, while the plague raged, services were held at Cucklet church, a dell south of the village. An annual commemorative service is held here in August. Another interesting tomb is that of the county cricketer, Henry Bagshaw, with a representation of a set of wickets and an umpire's hand, signifying the final 'out'.

At Eyam, join A6521 which looks down on Middleton Dale and Stoney Middleton. At B6001 turn left and keep on through **Grindleford** as A6521 to join A625 for Sheffield.

An extension of the route can be made from Grindleford. Turn left following B6001 for Hathersage and left again up Sir William Hill Road opposite the Sir William Hotel. The road rises to 1400 feet and has good views over the Highlow Brook and the Derwent Valley towards Hathersage —more disused lead mines line its route for we are now running over Eyam Moor. The 'Not Suitable for Motors' sign indicates the disused turnpike road of 1757 over Sir William Hill. After a short while turn right for Hucklow and Bretton. The view is now to the left looking down on Eyam. After passing the Barrel Inn at **Bretton** bear right, and further on right again up the hill which ascends Burrs Mount towards Abney. At the top is the field used by the Lancashire and Cheshire Gliding Club whose planes make use of the rising air currents above Hucklow Edge. The Northern Gliding Championships are held there in July and August. The road is narrow but picturesque, winding through **Abney,** a tiny hamlet looking across to Shatton Moor and Sir William Hill. It drops sharply toward Hathersage. On the right is the sixteenth-century Highlow Hall, with its stone dovecote. At B6001, opposite the Plough Inn, turn left, cross the Derwent and at the give-way opposite the George turn right. Sheffield is reached along A625 in twelve miles.

ROUTE 3

SHEFFIELD — Dronfield — Chesterfield — Matlock — Cromford — Grangemill — Alport — Youlgreave — Over Haddon — Bakewell — Stoney Middleton — Calver — Froggatt Edge — SHEFFIELD (55 miles).

Leave **Sheffield** by A61 for Dronfield and Chesterfield. **Dronfield** is reached in four miles. It was a prosperous market town during the Georgian period but was then industrialised. The early solid houses remain, surrounding the nineteenth-century additions. The Manor House is now the council offices. The fourteenth-century church has a Jacobean pulpit, an alabaster effigy and three brasses, one of them the only brass in England of two brothers, both of whom were priests. Continue along A61 to **Chesterfield** (see page 60), noting the silhouette of the crooked spire. From Chesterfield it is possible to divert to Barlborough (A619) (see page 57), Bolsover (A632) (page 58) or Hardwick (A617) (page 64), all sites of famous halls. Our route takes A632 for Matlock and the long pull from Chesterfield carries us away from the industrial area and on to the moors.

A road to the left leads to **Wingerworth** where amidst new housing stands an old church to which a modern nave (1964) has been added with great success. Abstract patterns of coloured glass contrast with the wall paintings, the plain Norman chancel and the font. Just past Kelstedge, A632

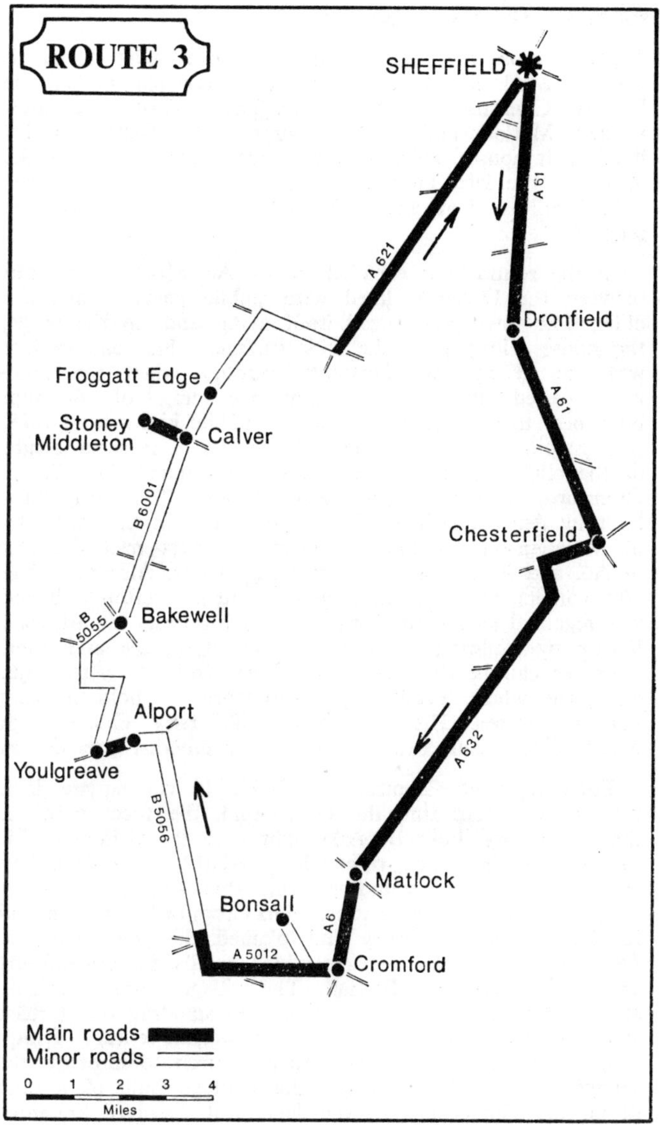

ROUTE 3
SHEFFIELD
Dronfield
A 61
A 61
A 621
Chesterfield
Froggatt Edge
Stoney Middleton
Calver
B 6001
A 632
Bakewell
B 5055
Alport
Youlgreave
B 5056
Matlock
Bonsall
A 6
A 5012
Cromford
Main roads
Minor roads
0 1 2 3 4
Miles

drops to cross the river Amber, then rises again to climb over to Matlock. Matlock Moor has been planted by the Forestry Commission with conifers. The road begins to drop towards Matlock and the deep gorge of the Derwent valley lined with houses. **Riber Castle** stands ominously across the valley to the left. Descend A632 into **Matlock** (avoid the 1 in 5 hill) and at A615 turn right towards the town (see page 65).

At the roundabout turn left along A6 which is confined between the Derwent, lined with public gardens, and the cliffs. The town has spread itself along and up the gorge, the houses clinging to the rock surface. This road in fact was created in the nineteenth century when the route was blasted through the limestone crag of Scarthin Nick near to Cromford. It became a public highway in 1818, thus helping the development of the spa. The sheer height of the cliff face shows the task of the undertaking. Before **Cromford,** are the red-brick Masson Mills. The early part, built by Arkwright in 1783, is recognisable in the centre by its Venetian-type windows. Arkwright's first mill lies east of A6, and is now a colour grinding works. Arkwright had 200 workers, many of them children, in his cotton mill and was regarded as a model employer for his time. He attracted labour by building good houses for employees and some examples can be seen in North Street (c.1777). Attics ran along the whole length of the top storey to hold stocking knitting frames. His own home, Willersley Castle, with pseudo-Gothic round towers, is now a Methodist guest-house.

Turn right at Cromford (A5012). In the square is a pleasant Georgian inn, the Greyhound, the focal point of the community, built by Arkwright to lodge visitors to his fine new mills. Turn right along A5012, Via Gellia. In spite of its Roman sounding name this was made by the Gell family who carved a route from Cromford to Grangemill in the nineteenth century and planted the trees along it. (At the Pig of Lead, a name which recalls the lead-mining era, a road leads to **Bonsall.** The village climbs the hill, at its centre a market cross (plate 13) standing on thirteen steps. It is overlooked by the seventeenth-century King's Head and the thirteenth-century church dominates the village.) Along the road is Tufa Cottage built of a kind of porous rock created by the deposit of dissolved limestone on moss.

A5012 runs through Middleton Wood and Hopton Wood. Unfortunately the valuable limestone is being exploited, especially that in Hoptonwood quarries. Turn right at **Grangemill,** by the Hollybush Inn, for Bakewell (B5056), traversing the winding road which runs between Harthill and Stanton Moors. Both these areas were inhabited in prehistoric times and evidence remains in the form of barrows and stone circles. Stanton Stone Circle can be approached by way of Birchover. At the give-way turn left towards **Alport** where the Lathkill meets the Bradford. Alport is a pleasant village with views across Lathkill Dale. A mill was recorded here in 1159 and there is still a picturesque one by the weir. Cross the bridge over the Lathkill built in 1718 to help trains of packhorses, and continue to **Youlgreave,** overlooking the Bradford. The church, with its massive square tower, dominates the village. It has an unusual font with a tiny bowl projecting from the mouth of a strange animal carved on the side of it. The font originally belonged to Elton which cast it out, but then wanted it back. Elton has had to be satisfied with a copy. There is a small alabaster tomb of Thomas Cockayne (died 1488), the sides and ends decorated with angels holding painted shields. His head rests on a cock. The east window is by Burne-Jones and another, the War Memorial Window, is composed of fragments of stained glass brought from Ypres Cathedral and other Belgian churches destroyed in World War I.

Turn right opposite the church (Conksbury Lane) to run through stone-wall country. At the give-way turn right and cross the Lathkill by the tiny Conksbury Bridge. This is the only point at which a road approaches **Lathkill Dale** though a walker can go from here to Over Haddon or to Alport. Climb out of the dale and take the next left turn to Over Haddon. Just before **Over Haddon** turn right for Bakewell. From the village there are good views over **Lathkill Dale** and a path descends to the ford. After a mile turn right (B5055) for **Bakewell** (see page 57). At the bottom of the hill, skirt the roundabout and take A619 for Chesterfield, cross the river, go up the hill to B6001 for Hathersage. **Hassop** station, built c.1863 to serve the Duke of Devonshire, is now a depot for agricultural machinery. After two miles the road winds past the high walls of the Eyre estate. The Jacobean house can be seen through the trees and the Roman Catholic chapel stands high above the road. Eventually we drop to Calver. To the left along A623 is Middleton Dale, a gorge of rocky heights, quarries and woodlands entered at

Stoney Middleton where houses built by miners and quarry-men rise in tiers up the hillside. The church has an octagonal nave of 1759 added to the fifteenth-century tower built by Joan Eyre in thankfulness for her husband's safe return from Agincourt. Nearby is a hot spring (63° F.) round which Lord Denman arranged some bathing buildings, no longer used.

Return to Calver and take B6001, then turn right (B6054) signposted to Sheffield by **Froggatt Edge.** The road crosses the Derwent and winds upwards while the village nestles at the foot of the Edge. The view extends across the Derwent, beyond Hathersage to Bamford Edge. At Totley Moss the road divides; keep right for Dronfield passing Barbrook Reservoir and the mosses of Big Moor. At the roundabout at Owler Bar keep left (A621) reaching Sheffield in six miles.

ROUTE 4

DERBY — Borrowash — Elvaston Castle — Aston-on-Trent — Weston-on-Trent — Swarkestone — Stanton-by-Bridge — Melbourne — Ticknall — Foremark — Repton — Hilton — Sudbury — Norbury — Yeaveley — Alkmonton — Longford — DERBY (55 miles).

Leave **Derby** (see page 61) on A52 towards Nottingham. At Spondon take A6005 from the roundabout towards Long Eaton. At the suburb of **Borrowash,** where the monks of Dale Abbey (plate 20) established their corn mills and, to the fury of the people of Derby, erected a weir which blocked navigation on the Derwent, turn right (B5010) towards Chellaston. The road passes **Elvaston Castle,** former home of the Stanhopes, earls of Harrington, and now a public park. The castle was remodelled by James Wyatt after 1817 but the landscaped gardens are more impressive, especially the topiary. The church holds monuments to the Stanhopes, the most imposing being the alabaster effigies of Sir John Stanhope (died 1610) and his wife.

A mile further turn left along A6 and immediately right towards **Aston-on-Trent.** We shall be travelling through the valley of the Trent for some time, although the river belongs to Derbyshire for only part of its course—it rises in Stafford-shire and passes through to Nottinghamshire. Aston Hall is now a hospital but the church survives, its most notable monument being a fifteenth-century alabaster tomb-chest. In the centre of the village turn right (Weston Road) for **Weston-on-Trent,** situated near the Leicestershire border, a more scattered village with the church some distance away. A lane leads to the bank of the Trent, opposite the King's Mill, where a skirmish was fought during the Civil War, and the dead lie buried in the churchyard. The font, pulpit and tower screen were fitted in 1661 to replace those damaged by Cromwell's soldiers. Unfortunately the slate gravestones are now arranged forlornly round the churchyard walls.

Continue to **Swarkestone** through intensively cultivated fields. At the give-way turn left over the Trent and Mersey Canal, which you will find running parallel to the Trent for this part of its course. Across the fields to the left is a curious building of two storeys with domed towers at each end. It is probably Jacobean and is said to have been either a summer-house or a grandstand for some sport. The church has two fine monuments to the Harpur family—Sir Richard (died 1577) in his judge's gown, and Sir John (died 1627) in armour. The family's best memorial is, however, the inn name, the Crewe and Harpur Arms. Join A514 going left for Melbourne and cross Swarkestone Bridge, first a graceful structure of five arches rebuilt in 1796, then a causeway

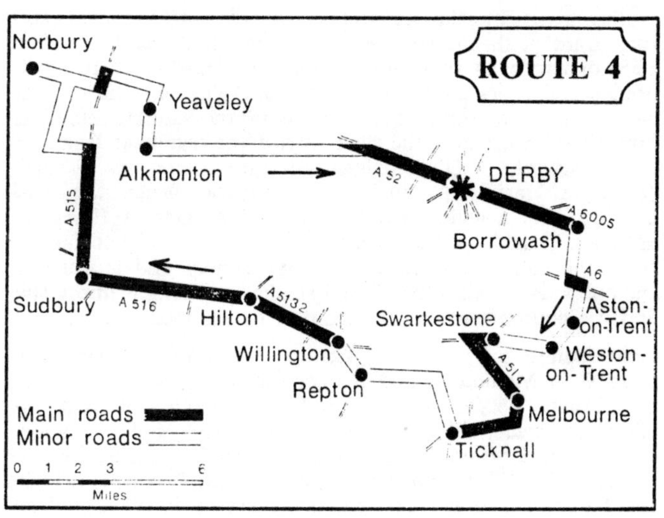

of seventeen arches over marshy ground, the longest medieval bridge in Britain. The Royalists tried to stop the Parliamentarians here in 1643 and over a hundred years later an advance guard of Prince Charles Edward's troops reached the bridge only to receive word to retreat. At the end the road rises to the millstone-grit beds on which lies **Stanton-by-Bridge**, whose church still has Saxon and Norman remains and a recess containing a stone effigy of a priest.

Keep on A514 then B587 for Melbourne. The land is extensively used for market-gardening, hence the almost hedgeless landscape. **Melbourne** is one of the oldest Derbyshire towns. The manor, mentioned in Domesday Book, belonged to the bishops of Carlisle, who probably financed the building of the huge Norman church. Later additions were made to it during the centuries but the most impressive part is the Norman nave with huge pillars and carved capitals. **Melbourne Hall** (open to the public), built about 1700, has an impressive garden laid out on the Dutch plan and includes a yew tunnel 180 feet long, and an ironwork arbour (c.1711) erected by Robert Bakewell of Derby. There are some pleasant buildings in the town including a group of fourteen cottages and a chapel built and endowed by Thomas Cook, founder of the travel agency.

Bear right by the nineteenth-century butter market and turn right at the Melbourne Arms towards **Ticknall**, reached after two miles, a small village with eighteenth-century almshouses and a Victorian-Gothic church. The old church was blown up; two parts of it remain in the churchyard. The horseshoe bridge over the road carried the tramroad from the old limeworks. Turn right in the centre of Ticknall (opposite Harpur Avenue) for **Foremark**. When the road drops, giving a wide view, turn left. The gates of Foremark Hall are passed — the former home of the Burdett family. Now the hall is Repton Preparatory School and is open to the public at certain times. The Palladian building is impressive and the church contains the Burdett family monuments.

At **Milton** turn right for **Repton** (plate 18), a town even older than Melbourne and the capital of the Saxon kingdom of Mercia. Peada, son of Penda of Mercia, brought his Christian bride, Elfleda, here in A.D. 653 and an abbey was founded seven years later, only to be sacked by the Danes in 874. The church was rebuilt about 970. Surprisingly the Normans did not destroy, but enlarged it. Though later additions have altered the fabric, the Saxon crypt has survived. The Saxon kings of Mercia were buried here and in 870 the burial of St. Wystan made it a centre of pilgrimage. The present crypt dates from a rebuilding in the tenth century. Nothing is left of the abbey, but the remains of a priory, founded in 1172 by Matilda, Countess of Chester, and dissolved in 1538, are incorporated into Repton School, which was founded soon after the Dissolution. The priory gateway and part of the cloisters remain but most of the school buildings belong to the nineteenth century.

At Repton turn right, circumnavigating the market cross, and proceed to **Willington** dominated by the huge power station. Cross the Trent over the five-arched bridge, go under the railway bridge and turn left (A5132) towards Hilton. The road rises by a new flyover to cross the Roman road, Rykneld Street, now the busy A38. Join A516 at **Hilton.** The route can be shortened here to return to Derby (7 miles) via **Etwall,** a pretty village with a fine church containing monuments of the Port family, including that of Sir John, founder of Repton School.

Turn left along A516 for Sudbury. Two miles further is **Hatton,** linked to **Tutbury** by a bridge and gazing up at those castle walls behind which Mary, Queen of Scots, pined for freedom. A516 joins A50 before **Sudbury,** where the picturesque inn, the Vernon Arms, built by George Vernon in 1671, commemorates a family who held the hall for 400 years. The hall (plate 15), begun in 1616 by Mary Vernon and finished by George Vernon between 1670-90, is a fine example of English Renaissance work. It is now the property of the National Trust and open to the public. The plaster work and wood carving are remarkable.

After Sudbury turn right (A515) for Ashbourne. Three miles further turn left, opposite the Howard Arms, for Marston Montgomery and at the first crossroads turn right for Norbury. At the end of the road, which emerges opposite the Queen Adelaide, turn left for **Norbury** church just over a mile away. This has a spacious chancel (1349-95) with fourteenth-century glass and two splendid alabaster tombs (plate 16). Sir Nicholas Fitzherbert in plate armour has his feet supported by a tiny angel, and Sir Ralph lies by his wife, while a bedesman prays at his feet. Their numerous progeny surround the tomb. The Georgian hall is by the side of the church. The medieval great hall is open to the public each Wednesday afternoon (May to September). George

Eliot set part of *Adam Bede* in this area.

Return to the Queen Adelaide and bear right for Cubley. Turn left at A515 then right to Yeaveley, crossing the runway of the disused aerodrome. Just over a mile further on bear right to **Yeaveley,** thought to be the birthplace of Henry Yevele, architect of the nave of Westminster Abbey. At Yeaveley go straight on. At **Alkmonton** turn left for Longford, passing the nineteenth-century church with a flint-stone wall, unusual for this part of the country. **Longford Hall,** whose facade dates from 1700, has been restored after being burned out in 1942 and can be seen across the park. A bridleway leads to the church containing tombs of the Longford family. Keep on for Derby. Soon the road is relatively straight, for it was the Roman road to the fort of Little Chester. At the give-way turn right (B5020) and after a mile keep straight on for Derby. **Mickleover** is to the right, consisting of some old houses amidst modern buildings. When the route meets A52 turn right for Derby.

ROUTE 5

DERBY — Ripley — South Wingfield — Crich — Cromford — Matlock — Darley Dale — Wensley — Winster — Elton — Brassington — Carsington — Hopton — Wirksworth — Belper — Duffield — Darley Abbey — DERBY (58 miles).

From **Derby** (see page 61) take A61 for nine miles to Ripley, a busy industrial town, especially so on Saturdays when the market is held. Beyond Swanwick, after the large roundabout turn left (A615) for Matlock. (Just ahead on A61 is **Alfreton** with some interesting houses set round a square, including the Georgian George Hotel. Opposite the post office is an Elizabethan house. The church dates from the twelfth to fifteenth centuries.) At the give-way turn left, then immediately right (B5053) for **South Wingfield.** The station here is of unusual design, built by the railway architect, Francis Thompson, but is now a private house. South Wingfield is an industrial village but over to the left can be seen the impressive remains of **Wingfield Manor.** This was begun by Ralph, Lord Cromwell, treasurer to Henry VI, who died before it was finished. It came into the possession of the earls of Shrewsbury and the sixth earl was the custodian of Mary, Queen of Scots, who was lodged here in 1569

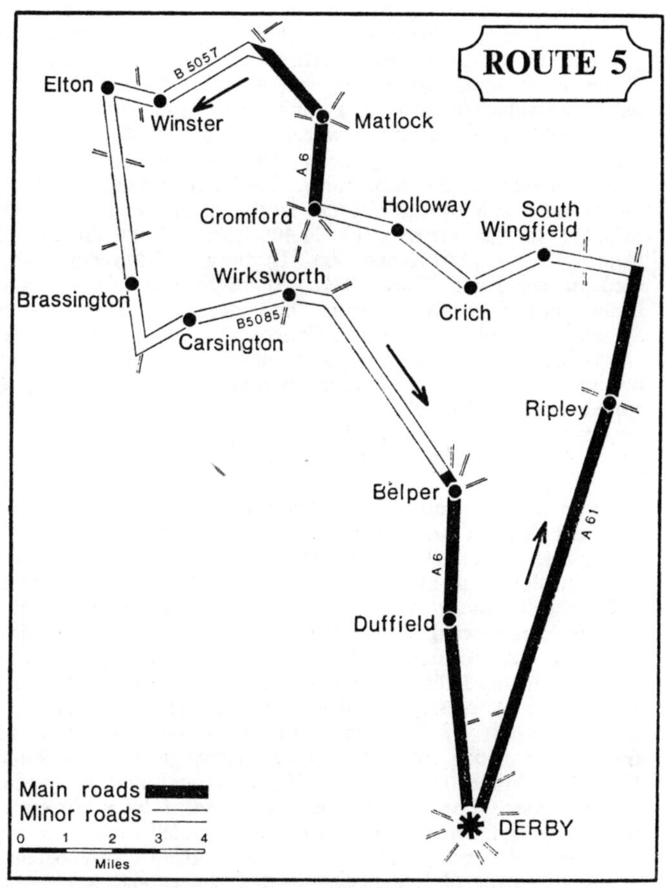

and again in 1584. In that year the unfortunate Anthony Babington, who had a house at Dethick four miles away, plotted to release her, was discovered and executed. During the Civil War the house was held first by the Parliamentarians, then by the Royalists, and was recaptured for Parliament by Sir John Gell with much damage. Decay and removal of stonework over the centuries have still not destroyed the majesty of the ruins.

Beyond South Wingfield is **Crich.** On the hill turn right by the restored market cross for Holloway. Just beyond is the church, of the fourteenth century but with Norman aisles. There is a carved oak screen and a stone effigy of William de Wakebridge dressed in a long gown and with a small angel holding a Catherine wheel to his ear. In the main street is a framework knitter's house distinguished by its long windows in the top storey. On **Crich Stand,** a superb viewpoint north of the church, is the memorial tower built in 1923 to the memory of 11,400 men of the Sherwood Foresters (the Nottingham and Derbyshire Regiment) who died in the First World War. At night the beacon light flashes out over five counties and over the memorial to Sir Horace Lockwood Smith-Dorrien. The tower stands above Crich quarry which was dug by George Stevenson to provide lime for his kilns at Ambergate. Quarrying has now ceased and, within the quarry, is the **Tramway Museum** housing a collection of old trams and tramway equipment (plate 19). Tram rides can be taken round the quarry.

From Crich continue to **Holloway,** which overlooks the Derwent Valley, and then drop down towards **Cromford.** The estate on the left is **Lea Hurst,** the house where Florence Nightingale lived as a child and to which she returned after the Crimean War, quietly and alone, avoiding the civic welcome awaiting her. The house is now an old people's home. At the bottom of the hill the road swings to follow the Derwent and the Cromford Canal; road, river, canal and railway are all pressed together in this gorge. The canal was dug (1788-93) by William Jessup to provide a means of tranporting goods for Sir Richard Arkwright. In 1900 the Butterley Tunnel collapsed cutting the canal and its useful life was over. The road crosses the Derwent by a fifteenth-century bridge with the peculiarity of rounded arches on the upstream side and pointed on the downstream. Just beyond is the basement of a medieval bridge chapel and a decayed eighteenth-century fishing house inscribed *'Piscatoribus sacrum'.* The church was built by Richard Arkwright in 1797 on the site of an earlier lead-smelting mill.

At the A6 turn right for Matlock. The red-brick Masson Mills incorporate Arkwright's original building of 1783. Keep on through **Matlock** (see page 65) and at the roundabout bear left for Bakewell. Two miles on is **Darley Dale,** whose centre is Church Town, just west of A6. St. Helen's Church was extended between the twelfth and fifteenth centuries. The window in the south transept is attributed to Burne-Jones. Inside are some interesting monuments and the churchyard contains a vast yew tree, at least 1400 years old and with a girth of 33 feet, and several unusual table tombs dating from the Stuart period; one has carvings of a weaver's loom. Just past St. Elphin's girls' school turn left for Winster; at the give-way go left again (B5057). Ascend the hill towards **Wensley** and keep on for **Winster,** a compact town, bearing evidence of eighteenth-century prosperity from its lead-mining. The old hall has giant pilasters and a balustraded parapet. For a time it belonged to Llewellyn Jewitt, a historian of Derbyshire. The seventeenth-century market hall was the first property in Derbyshire to be acquired by the National Trust. The church has a Norman font but more unusual is the nave, which is divided down the middle by an arcade. There is a representation of Leonardo da Vinci's *Last Supper* in cast iron, a versatile though bizarre feat. On each Shrove Tuesday the villagers compete in pancake races.

Bear right at the end of Winster and at the give-way cross the main road and go towards **Elton,** a village which was equally prosperous in the eighteenth century. Some older buildings remain; the Old Hall is now a Youth Hostel. In Elton turn sharp left at the church (by the Duke of York) and half a mile on take the right fork for Aldwark through characteristic stone-wall country. At the next two give-ways go straight on, then keep right for Brassington running beneath Minninglow, crowned by a tumulus and crossed by a Roman road. At the give-way, cross B5056. On the left is Longcliffe quarry. The bridge across the road carried the Cromford and High Peak Railway. The road begins to drop towards **Brassington.** The village is generally undistinguished but the composition of local styles of architecture, much of it dating from the seventeenth and eighteenth centuries, is typical of the area. This is the last of the 'stone' villages for we are now leaving the upland area for the lower land. St. James's Church has remains of Norman work including the west tower and the chancel. Compare the Norman piers of the south aisle wall and those of the Victorian north aisle. The countryside is full of prehistoric remains while the number of disused lead mines shows its eighteenth-century importance. Go south through Brassington and at B5035 turn left for Wirksworth.

Carsington ranges up the valley side, the houses arranged in tiers. The small church appears to be Gothic but was built in 1648. The windows are in memory of the Gells of Hopton. One contains the names of all the women, from 1452 to 1862, the other the men, from 1404 to 1926. The road passes the home of the Gells, **Hopton Hall,** recognisable by the undulating brick wall. Beyond are the almshouses endowed by Sir Philip in 1722. A steep hill descends into **Wirksworth** (see page 67). At the give-way turn left and immediately right continuing along B5035 towards Alfreton. As we pull up the hill the view reveals Wirksworth, dominated by the vast quarry carved out in the hillside.

At the Malt Shovel, instead of swinging left with the main road, bear right for Belper, along a road overlooking the limestone ravine of the Derwent Valley towards the Crich Tower. Roads on the right lead to Alport Hill, the highest viewpoint in Derbyshire, owned by the National Trust. Alderwasley off to the left has good views of the valley and Shining Cliff Woods. Keep on for Belper and at the Bull's Head turn left, rising first, then dropping into Belper. At the give-way bear left along A517 which enters **Belper** (see page 58) by the rebuilt Strutt mills (now English Sewing Ltd.), a gaunt mass of red brick. Turn right along A6 passing the Brettle Mills built in 1834 in a dignified style.

After four miles **Duffield** is reached, some fine houses, an Elizabethan hall and a Baptist chapel of 1830. The church, mainly fourteenth century, is by the river. Inside is the alabaster tomb of Sir Roger Mynors and his wife, and a wall monument to Anthony Bradshaw, his two wives and twenty children.

Keep on for Derby along A6. Just before Derby is **Darley Abbey,** the site of the medieval priory of Austin Canons dissolved in 1539. The grounds are now a public park and of the former glory nothing remains but pieces of walling built into later houses. Cotton and paper mills were founded here in 1783 by Thomas Evans. The cotton mill was burnt down in 1788 but was rebuilt immediately. This still survives, together with the weir and toll-bridge over the river, maintained by the company. Derby is entered in two miles.

1. *The toll-house on the old bridge at Baslow (Route 1).*

2. *The wrought iron entrance gate at Chatsworth is possibly the work of Gardom (Route 1).*

3. *The Grand Cascade at Chatsworth was designed by Thomas Archer in 1696 for the formal gardens, prior to Capability Brown's alterations (Route 1).*

4. *The seventeenth-century Tissington Hall, home of the Fitzherbert family for 400 years (Routes 1 and 8).*

5. *The stepping stones across the river in Dovedale, perhaps the most beautiful of all the dales (Routes 1, 6 and 8).*

6. *A delightful Derbyshire custom is well dressing. As in this example at Hope flower petals are pressed on to a clay base to form a biblical scene (Route 2).*

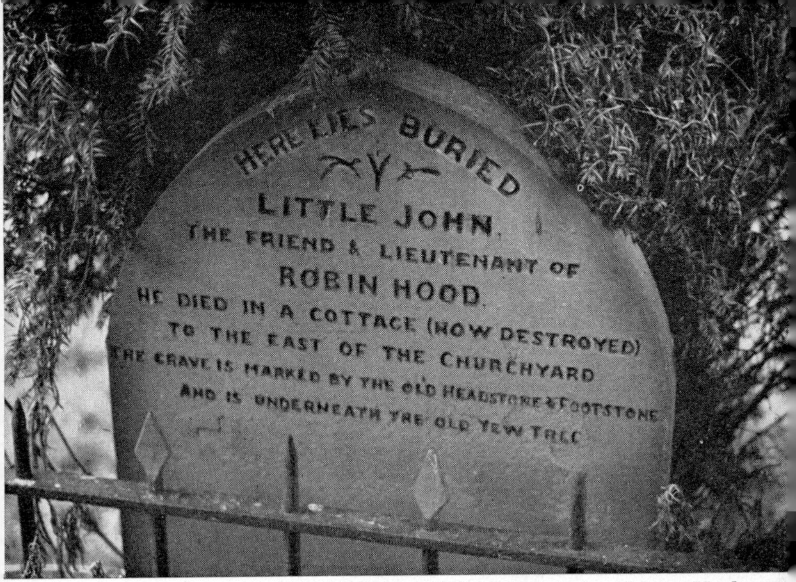

7. *Little John was born and is buried, it is said, at Hathersage where he returned after the death of his leader, Robin Hood (Route 2).*

8. *At Castleton on 29th May, Garland Day, a man representing Charles II rides through the village wearing a bell-shaped garland (Route 2).*

9. Peveril Castle near Castleton was built by William Peveril, one of the Conqueror's followers, but the keep dates from 1176 (Route 2).

10. The Crescent at Buxton, 200 yards long, was designed by John Carr in 1784, when the fifth Duke of Devonshire was developing the town as a spa (Routes 2, 7, 8 and 9).

11. *This late eighteenth-century sundial on the wall of Eyam church gives the time in such widespread places as Panama and Isfahan (Route 2).*

DERBYSHIRE
and the PEAK DISTRICT
M 1
M 18
SHEFFIELD
Glossop
A 624
A 57
Hayfield
A 5002
A 625
Hathersage
Eckington
A 616
Whaley Bridge
Chapel-en-
le-Frith
A 623
A 621
Dronfield
A 61
A 619
A 618
BUXTON
A 6
Chesterfield
A 632
Bolsover
Bakewell
A 617
Longnor
A 515
A 61
A 632
Matlock

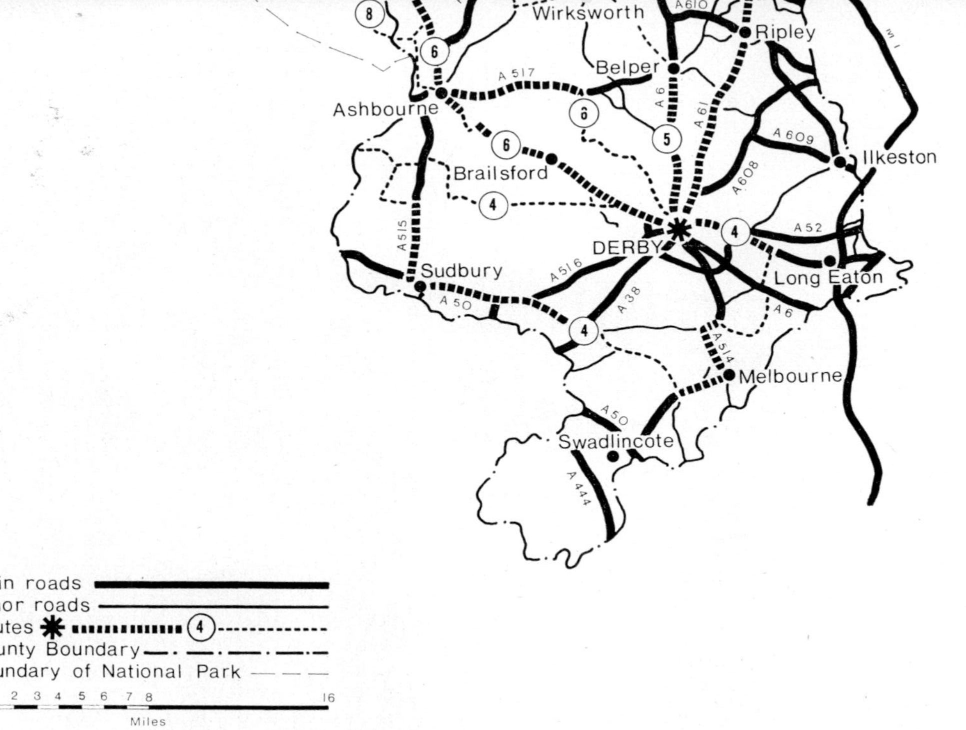

Wirksworth
A 610
Ripley
8
6
A 517
Belper
A 6
6
A 61
5
A 609
Ashbourne
Ilkeston
6
A 608
Brailsford
4
A 52
DERBY
4
A 515
A 516
Sudbury
A 38
Long Eaton
A 50
4
A 6
A 514
Melbourne
A 50
Swadlincote
A 444

Main roads
Minor roads
Routes
4
County Boundary
Boundary of National Park
0 1 2 3 4 5 6 7 8   16
Miles

12. *The crooked spire of the parish church of Chesterfield. The 228-foot spire leans almost 8 feet as a result of warping wood (Route 3).*

13. *The impressive market cross at the centre of Bonsall (Route 3).*

14. *All Saints church in Derby became the cathedral in 1927. It was rebuilt by James Gibbs in 1723, but the tower is the original in the Perpendicular style (Routes 4, 5 and 6).*

15. Sudbury Hall was built during the seventeenth century and was the home of Queen Adelaide after the death of her husband, William 1V (Route 4).

16. The finely decorated tomb of Sir Ralph Fitzherbert and his wife in Norbury church (Route 4).

17. The ninth-century
     Saxon cross in the
     churchyard at Eyam.
     The upper part of the
     shaft is missing (Route
     2).

18. The market cross and
     church at Repton. The
     Church still contains much
     Anglo-Saxon work, in-
     cluding the thousand-year-
     old crypt, but the spire is
     medieval (Route 4).

SANDEMAN'S PORTS
THE FINEST IN THE WORLD

19. This 1873 horse tram was built in Birkenhead, served
     in Portugal, and is now on display at the Crich Tramway
     Museum (Route 5).

20. The arch of the east window is all that remains of Dale
     Abbey, built on the site of a hermitage north-east of
     Derby.

21. *The remote Cat and Fiddle Inn near the Cheshire border not far from Buxton is 1690 feet above sea level (Route 7).*

DERBY — Kedleston — Weston Underwood — Ashbourne — Thorpe — Dovedale — Ilam — Alstonefield — Hulme End — Longnor — Fenny Bentley — Ashbourne — DERBY (60 miles).

Take A6 north out of **Derby** (see page 61) but branch off for Quarndon (Kedleston Road). At the next roundabout proceed for Quarndon. **Markeaton Park,** now owned by Derby Corporation, once belonged to the Mundys. Opposite are the modern buildings of Derby College of Art and Technology (1959). At Quarndon bear left for **Kedleston** and Hulland. **Kedleston Hall** (open during the summer on Sunday afternoons) has been the home of the Scarsdale family for 800 years, its most famous inhabitant being George Nathaniel, Marquess Curzon of Kedleston. The building, begun in 1758, has a north front, adorned with a vast portico and two wings added by James Paine, but Robert Adam took the Roman arch as a motif for the south front facing the gardens. Adam designed some rooms including the magnificent great hall, its roof supported by twenty Corinthian columns, the library, drawing room, staircase and state bedrooms, all elaborately decorated. All Saints' Church is a medieval structure with a nineteenth-century north aisle. The Curzon family monuments include the tomb chest of Sir John (died 1456) and his wife Joan, and the elaborate white marble tomb of Lord Curzon of Kedleston, dressed in his robes as Grand Master of the Star of India, lying by his first wife.

Continue as signposted for Weston Underwood and Hulland. From Weston a road on the left leads to **Mugginton** whose church, standing high above the tiny village, has a Norman tower. An epitaph mentions Hugh Radcliffe who died in 1678, 'sometime haberdasher of hats to his late Majesty and all his royal family'. In the south chapel is the tomb of Sir Nicholas Kniverton and his wife who died about 1400 but their brasses, together with the tiny ones of their children, are of 75 years later. In the vicinity is Halter Devil Chapel, attached to a farmhouse. In 1723 Francis Brown swore to ride to Derby even if he had to halter the Devil. He threw the halter over the 'horse', found he was putting it on horns and fainted as a clap of thunder rang out. A reformed man, he built the chapel as an act of repentance. One wonders—had he tried to harness a cow?

Pass through Weston Underwood and two and a half miles on, bear left for **Hulland Ward,** then follow the signs for Ashbourne. The countryside is pleasantly wooded although parts of this area are being quarried for gravel. The hills rise in the distance. At **Ashbourne** (see page 56) take A515 for Buxton and Dovedale, and soon turn left for Dovedale. The millstone marks the entrance to the National Park, and already **Thorpe Cloud** and Bunster Hill are in view. Turn left at the Dog and Partridge. Soon a splendid view of the dale appears, the two peaks guarding the entrance. Cross the two bridges over the Dove. The entrance to **Dovedale** (see page 62) appears on the right.

The road runs by the river Manifold to **Ilam.** Bear right here and right again climbing out of the valley. Soon we are in stone-wall country with its familiar pattern of enclosure. After three miles turn right dropping down to **Hope** and immediately rising to **Alstonefield** whose church was mentioned by Charles Cotton in the section which he wrote for the *Compleat Angler.* Bear left for Hartington and Hulme End. To the left is Top of Ecton. Ecton mines once produced copper which was taken to Hartington. When the Manifold Railway was constructed it was hoped that this would revive the mining industry but these were false hopes. Keep on for **Hulme End** with a wide view of the Manifold Valley in front. At the give-way by the Light Railway Hotel turn left (B5054). The green sheds are the terminus of the former railway and from this point a walk can be taken along the track to the **Manifold Valley** (see page 65). One mile further turn right along B5053. The view to the right looks across the upper stretches of the Manifold Valley to the stone walls beyond. Eventually the road climbs to the moorland village of **Longnor,** grouped like an embattled fortress on the ridge between Dove and Manifold. At the village turn right into the square where the Victorian market hall faces the Crewe and Harpur Arms. The eighteenth-century interior of the church belies its grim exterior. A quarter of a mile further descend into the valley of the Dove. Over to the left are Harkhouse Hill and the moors of Axe Edge.

Since Ilam we have been in the Staffordshire part of the Peak District but crossing the Dove brings us back into Derbyshire at the tiny village of **Crowdecote.** The road winds up steeply, revealing behind us more and more of the Dove Valley. Almost at the top on the right is a small dewpond; on the left small quarries line the road. The undulating road continues and swoops down towards the Royal Oak at **Hurdlow**. At the give-way turn right along A515. The track of the Cromford and High Peak Railway can be seen. It was the only railway in the country which was built to connect two canals—the Cromford Canal in the Derwent Valley and the Peak Forest Canal at Whaley Bridge. As such its stations were called wharves. It rose 990 feet from Cromford by a series of inclines, with gradients as steep as 1 in 7, to 1268 feet, reaching its highest point near the group of cottages known as **Parsley Hey.** Just beyond here the cutting can be seen on the left and the road crosses a small tunnel with excellent dressed limestone blocks. There are interesting medallions of the railway company at each end. Passengers were carried between 1855 and 1877 but traffic declined and the main freight was crushed limestone. The

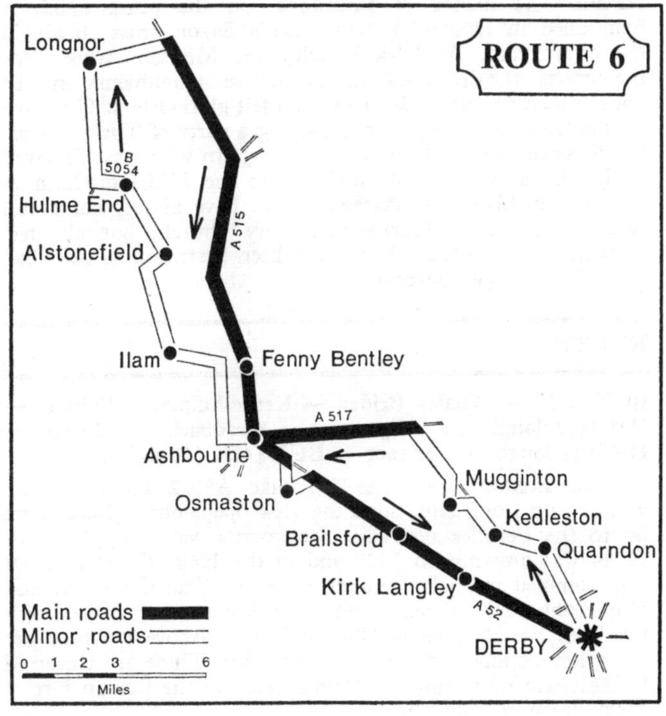

rails were removed some years ago and 18 miles of the track are being developed as the High Peak Trail.

The Roman road from Buxton to Little Chester ran to the left of the modern road. Keep on A515 to **Fenny Bentley**. Turn right into Ashes Lane to see the church. The old Hall, home of the Beresfords, on the main road, was built by Sir Thomas after his return from Agincourt, where he had fought with his father and seven brothers. His tomb is in the church, an unusual design, for he and his wife lie packaged in their shrouds, tied head and foot, their 21 children, also shrouded, surrounding them. Opposite the church are modern cottages built in traditional stone.

Continue for Ashbourne, then take A52 for Derby. **Osmaston** lies off to the right, a manorial village created in the 1840s, but the manor-house has gone and only the Victorian cottages remain. The manor of **Brailsford**, on the other hand, is mentioned in Domesday Book and a Saxon cross stands in the churchyard. At **Kirk Langley** the Meynell Arms commemorates the Meynell family whose monuments in the church include one to William 'who fell gloriously at Guergivo on the Danube while gallantly leading a party of Turks against the Russians' in 1854 and another to John who was 'deprived of life by a collision of carriages on the Midland Counties Railway in 1851'. At **Mackworth** we have almost come full circle. There is a fourteenth-century church, but all that remains of the castle, said to have been destroyed in the Civil War, is its stone gatehouse.

ROUTE 7

BUXTON — Whaley Bridge — Kettleshulme — Rainow — Wildboarclough — Allgreave — Gradbach — Flash — Hollingsclough — Longnor — BUXTON (40 miles).

From **Buxton** (see page 59) take A5002 for Stockport winding up Long Hill. Soon the view opens out to look down on to the Fernilee reservoir, Stockport's water supply. This valley was drowned in 1923 and in the 1960s the river Goyt was dammed to make another reservoir. The Cromford and High Peak Railway ran along the valley to its junction with the Peak Forest canal at Whaley Bridge. Above the road are the gritstone moors rising to Black Edge. These are traversed by a Roman route running from Buxton to the Roman fort of Melandra near Glossop.

Descend to **Whaley Bridge,** an old cotton town which takes its name from the bridge crossing the Goyt, a feature which appears on its coat of arms. Yet another reservoir is here, Toddbrook Reservoir built to serve the needs of the Peak Forest Canal. Above the town is the curious Roosdyche, a valley carved out in the Ice Age, about half a mile long. Legend said that it was a Roman racecourse but it is now accepted as a natural phenomenon. Turn left (traffic lights) for Macclesfield. (Off to the left is **Taxal,** a small village which overlooks the Goyt valley and across to Kinder Scout. In the church is a memorial to Michael Heathcote, 'Gentleman of the Pantry and Yeoman of the Mouth to his late Majesty King George the Second'. As he lived to be 73 his tasting of the king's food did him no harm.)

Keep on for Macclesfield. **Kettleshulme** was famous for its candlewick factory (closed in 1937). The road winds through

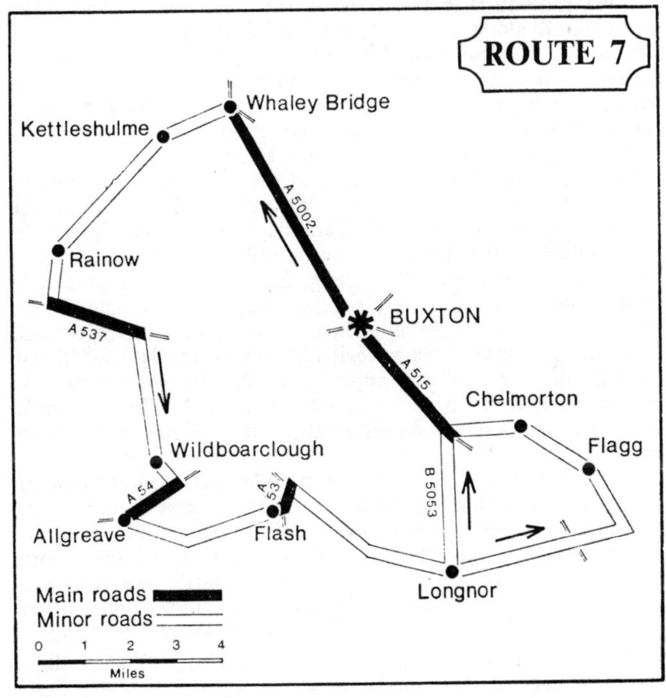

the hills to **Rainow,** a group of old cottages and a modern church. The road can be bleak in winter but autumnal tints give a scenic beauty. Just past the Rising Sun turn left along Penny Lane, the westernmost boundary of the National Park, and at its end turn left for Buxton along A537. At **Walker Barn** the Setter Dog is a rendezvous for hikers. One mile further turn right at the crossroads for Wildboarclough and keep right at the Stanley Arms. On the hills, far to the left, is the remote Cat and Fiddle, 1690 feet above sea level (plate 21). **Wildboarclough,** a narrow wooded glen, runs southwards, the most westerly valley of the National Park. A road leads to **Forest Chapel,** where the rush-bearing service is held in August. At the row of cottages, which is the village of Wildboarclough, turn left, cross the river, pass the large post office and climb alongside the wall of Crag Hall. Keep right up the hill and at the give-way turn right along A54.

One mile further bear left at the Rose and Crown. The road winds along the upper reaches of the river Dane which it crosses at **Gradbach** Methodist chapel, built in 1849 to serve a thriving community working in the silk mill lower down the river. When water power ceased to be a practical proposition the mill closed and the congregation dwindled. A short walk away is Lud Church, a cleft in the rock, reputed to be the meeting place of Lollards in the early fifteenth century. Meetings ended when soldiers attacked and in the foray the beautiful grand-daughter of Walter de Ludawk was shot. The road climbs to **Flash,** proudly announcing itself to be 1518 feet above sea level. 'Flash' is slang for counterfeit money and as the name implies it was once a village of ill repute. Three Shires Head near here, where Derbyshire, Cheshire and Staffordshire meet, was a veritable den of thieves. When the Sheriff of one County approached the thieves crossed to another. It would be very unlikely that three Sheriffs would appear at the same time, although eventually the thieves were rooted out. At the give-way turn left and take the next turn right at the Travellers Rest. Keep right and then straight on along this moorland road which runs through heather and gorse, giving views of stone-wall country all round. In winter after a fall of snow the air will be crisp and clear, giving wide white views on each side. Unfortunately the road will most likely be impassable, as indeed will most of this route. After three miles at the halt sign two routes are possible.

For the shorter (5 miles) turn left along B5053, climb the hill and run by Nab End which looks across the Dove

Valley to the weirdly-shaped Aldery Cliff and High Wheeldon, the latter owned by the National Trust, a memorial to the men of the Staffordshire and Derbyshire Regiments who fell in the Second World War. The road drops sharply to cross the river at **Glutton Bridge,** passes a pleasantly proportioned house on the left dating from 1675 and goes through a narrow defile. Here is a close-up view of jointing in the limestone. In winter if the water in the joints freezes and expands this action can start to split the rock into vertical formations and any rock breaking off collects at the bottom. At the crossroads keep straight on. (The left leads through a remote valley to A53. The right leads to **Earl Sterndale,** a small village with a tiny green. The inn is the Quiet Woman and the signboard shows why.) Continue along B5053 winding upwards then dropping to Brierlow Bar, through the dusty area of the nearby quarry. This road is the same colour as were many in the eighteenth century when Thomas Telford started to surface his roads with small pieces of limestone. Travellers held up tinted glass to shield their eyes from the white glare. Turn left at A515 for Buxton.

For the longer route (13 miles) turn right to drop to the crossroads in the centre of **Longnor.** Turn left, then soon bear left again dropping towards **Crowdecote.** Climb the hill and continue until A515 is reached. Cross over heading for Monyash (B5055), once the lead-mining capital of the Peak. Turn left at the cross-roads in the village, then keep left for Flagg. In almost a mile keep left, then left again. **Flagg** is a typical upland village, its houses widely spaced, which comes alive once a year on Tuesday in Easter week for its point-to-point races. In 1947 it was cut off for seven weeks by huge drifts of snow. At the chapel bear right and turn left at the give-way for Chelmorton. **Chelmorton** is to the right, one main street set amongst enclosures. The narrow fields indicate early enclosure, the wider areas later ones. The medieval church under the hill, is filled with ancient coffin stones and has a rare fifteenth-century chancel screen. At the give-way turn left for Buxton. As the road climbs towards A515 Horseshoe Dale with steep sides cut back by water-flow can be seen to the right. At A515 turn right for Buxton.

BUXTON — Warslow — Hulme End — Alstonefield — Ilam — Dovedale — Thorpe — Tissington — Monyash — Taddington — BUXTON (40 miles).

Leave **Buxton** (see page 59) along A53 for Leek, steadily climbing towards the moors. Axe Edge Moor to the right contains the sources of the rivers Dove and Dane while the Manifold rises to the left. An extensive view shows not only the extent of the Dove Valley but also the characteristic landscape of the Peak, open country criss-crossed by stone walls and cut into by swift streams which leave the harder rock rearing up as escarpments and peaks. Here too can be seen one of the problems of the Peak, how to reconcile the demands of industry with the preservation of a National Park. The carboniferous limestone is very pure in its calcium carbonate content and this is vital to modern industry. The quarries, scarring the landscape, are excluded from the National Park. As the demand for lime grows so does the size of the quarry and disfigurement of the countryside increases apace. Defacement cannot be limited to the area round the quarry for it affects the distant scene; the Brierlow Bar quarries produce a dense smoke which can be seen for miles.

Keep on A53, across which sheep wander freely, for nearly eight miles and, as the road drops towards the Roaches, turn left for Warslow. This road runs through the army firing ranges which are at times in use. The terrain is bleak and wild, but is tinted in autumn by heather. In one mile keep right, signposted Leek. To the right the horizon is broken by the Roaches and Ramshaw Rocks, rising to 1654 feet, lying like a sleeping dinosaur, guarding the edge of the Park. The rocks are ideal for rock-climbing novices, while distant Tittesworth Reservoir provides water for Leek and fishing for anglers. Leek lies in the hollow. After a mile bear left for Warslow by the Mermaid Pool and cross the next junction. From the road we can look northward to the Manifold Valley and Longnor and southwards across Warslow Brook to Butterton and Grindon Moors. Go over the crossroads, bear right and drop down to **Warslow,** a gritstone village.

At the main road turn left and take the second turn right (B5054) for Hartington. Hedges and pastures have replaced moors and mosses. On entering Hulme End cross the bridge over the Manifold and immediately turn right by the Light

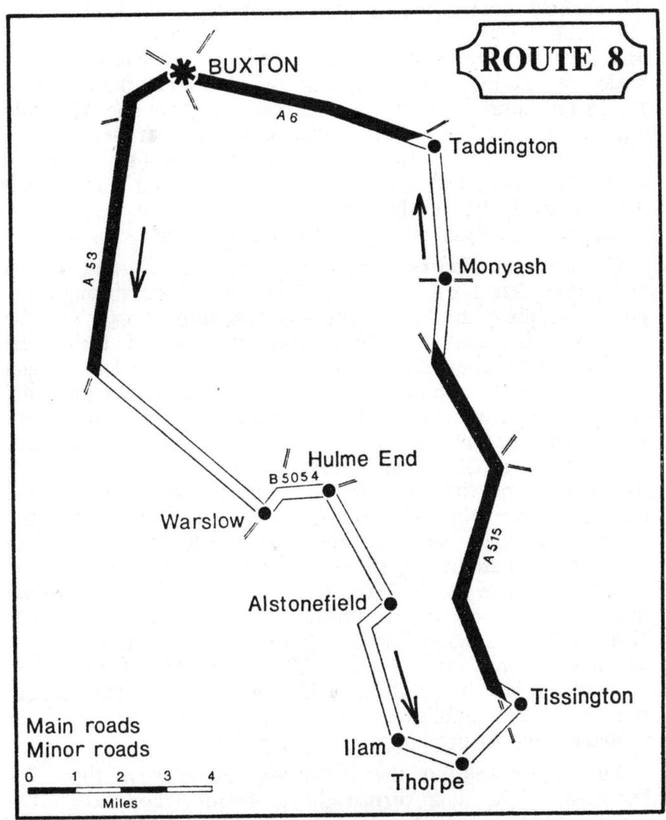

Railway Inn towards Alstonefield. **Hulme End** was the terminus of the Leek and Manifold Light Railway, completed in 1904 to carry passengers, minerals and dairy produce. Unfortunately, although it passed through some of the most scenic country, attracting sightseers and walkers, it never attracted enough freight to be profitable. In 1934 the track was closed and converted to a public footpath, which, as it provides the only route through part of the valley, is a valuable asset (see page 65).

On leaving Hulme End we are back in stone-wall country looking eastward over Beresford and Wolfscote Dales. At

Alstonefield by the village pump bear right and right again dropping towards Hopedale. Turn right, then take a sharp left turn for Dovedale. A deep gash to the left marks the Dale, carved into the surface of the limestone plateau. Our road runs along the watershed between the Dove and Manifold valleys. Descend the hill towards **Ilam,** bear left at the 'Eleanor Cross', pass the entrance of **Dovedale** (see page 62), cross the two bridges and climb to **Thorpe** up a slope which gives a good idea of the round contours of the valley sides, made by the action of running water over the centuries.

Go through Thorpe and at the Dog and Partridge turn right then left for Tissington. Cross A515, go through the gates and along the lime avenue to **Tissington** (page 7). The park was laid out by the Fitzherberts, one of the oldest Derbyshire families. At the end of the park turn left to pass the Hall Well opposite the gates of the hall (plate 4). At the end of the village keep left and at A515 turn right. On either side are drystone walls enclosing the fields. Until 100 years ago sheep and dairy farming was of primary importance and the enclosures were necessary to fence in the animals. Since then the number of sheep and cattle has steadily declined so that the patchwork effect is more picturesque than useful, though many fields are cropped for hay. The course of the Ashbourne — Buxton railway which once helped to move the produce can be seen on the left. Until 1795 the stage for post-horses on this turnpike road was a very long one — 21 miles. The **Newhaven Hotel** is the 'capital' inn which the Duke of Devonshire established, on the site of an old public house, so that post-horses could be provided here to break up the long stage.

Two miles beyond the Newhaven Hotel bear right for Monyash. (The next turn right leads to Arbor Low.) On entering **Monyash** notice the typical limestone houses with roofing flags, and door and window lintels of the more durable millstone grit. In medieval times limestone was being burned in this area to provide a fertiliser for the soil. One old kiln was excavated at Monyash in 1964 and a model of it is in Derby Museum. Keep straight on for Taddington at the crossroads, keep left at the junction following and right at the next. At the second give-way cross the Buxton — Bakewell secondary road and descend towards Taddington. Taddington Woods are under the protection of the National Trust as a valuable example of ashwoods in their natural state. **Taddington** is a good example of a street village, originally consisting of farms along a lane with later infilling. It looks north towards Miller's Dale. A footpath leads to **Five Wells Tumulus** where Neolithic people, the earliest inhabitants of the area, buried their dead. At an altitude of 1400 feet it is the highest megalithic monument in England. The churchyard cross may be Saxon or Norman and the medieval church (restored 1891) contains a brass of Sir Richard Blackwall with his wife, six sons and five daughters, and a rare stone gospel lectern projecting from the north wall of the chancel.

At the main road turn left along A6, a busy road confined by Wyedale and Ashdale. This descends past the quarries and leads back to Buxton beside the Wye.

ROUTE 9

BUXTON — Miller's Dale — Tideswell — Bradwell — Brough — Bamford — Ladybower Reservoir — Derwent Valley — Glossop — Hayfield — Chapel-en-le-Frith — BUXTON (53 miles).

Leave **Buxton** (see page 59) along A6 towards Matlock, a road which follows the windings of the Wye for three miles before climbing on to the limestone plateau. Turn left along B6049 for **Miller's Dale** and **Tideswell** (page 66). After Tideswell cross A623 and continue along B6049. There is a good view of Hucklow Edge, rising above **Great Hucklow.** Gliders often soar above it from the gliding field on the top of Abney Moor. Hucklow Edge continues as Bradwell Edge, a precipitous slope of millstone grit at the edge of the moorland. At the beginning of Bradwell Dale is **Hazlebadge Hall,** a sixteenth-century farmhouse which was part of the dowry which Dorothy Vernon brought to her husband, Sir John Manners. **Bradwell** has a Victorian church and houses rising up the slopes of the dale. Off to the left is Bagshaw Cavern which has fine crystalline formations. It is reached by a flight of 103 steps. Just before **Brough** a footpath leads to the site of the Roman fort of Anavio. Excavations have shown that it was occupied in the second century. Excavations on a larger scale are eating away the nearby landscape to provide cement for twentieth-century needs.

At the Traveller's Rest turn right (A625) and after a mile turn left (A6013) and left again past **Bamford** station which serves commuters to Sheffield and walkers to the moors. The village straggles up the hill. The church was built in Victorian Gothic style by William Butterfield. The road now runs between the drop of the Derwent valley and the heights of Bamford Edge. Soon the **Ladybower Reservoir** appears. The northern part of the National Park, composed of impervious gritstone, is the catchment area for the water supply of Sheffield, Leicester, Nottingham and Derby. In 1899 the Derwent Valley Water Board was formed to develop the resources of the area. Eventually three reservoirs were constructed, the first, the most northerly, is the **Howden Reservoir** (1912), the next the **Derwent** (1916), and the last Ladybower (1945) which submerged the villages of Ashopton and Derwent. During the drought of 1959 Derwent was exposed and opportunity was taken to demolish the church spire which had remained above the water. The Ladybower holds 6300 million gallons and is the largest in Britain, 1250 feet long. Man has altered the landscape with drastic but not unpleasing results.

Cross the viaduct over the reservoir and turn left along A57 for Glossop. (After the next viaduct a right turn leads along the Derwent and Howden Reservoirs for seven miles, a very fine run. The Derwent forms the boundary with Yorkshire for most of the upper course to the reservoir. Much of the area is planted with conifers to assist in regulating the flow of water.) A57 runs by the Ladybower, then follows the Woodlands Valley winding upwards towards the open moors. The road was originally laid out (1818-20) by Thomas Telford as a turnpike road linking Manchester and Sheffield. The **Snake Inn** marks the beginning of wooded Lady Clough, and the wildest and most scenic part begins; Kinder Scout lies to the South and aptly named Bleaklow to the north. Posts mark the route for the Snake Pass is usually snow bound in winter. Paths cross the wilderness including the Pennine Way and Doctor's Gate, a Roman road coming from Glossop. The highest point is 1680 feet and then the road descends by swinging round in wide curves. Glossop and the outlying industrial scene lie below but the view is partly hidden by the necessary crash barriers. The purple-clad moors give place to green fields as **Glossop** is reached (see page 63).

At the traffic lights turn left along A624 for Chapel-en-le-Frith. There is a steady climb to the Moors for three miles. This was the old route from Manchester to Buxton which took from seven to nine hours. In winter it was impassable. It is not surprising that the first Turnpike Act passed in

Derbyshire (1725) applied to this road and led to a general improvement. When the drop begins **Hayfield** lies below, factory chimneys dominating gritstone houses. This is a favourite starting point for walking to Kinder Scout by a rough track leading from the Royal Hotel via Farlands Booth. Another walk is to Chinley Churn (1480 feet) which gives good views towards industrial Stockport or menacing Kinder. A6015 leads from Heywood to **New Mills** (page 66) but keep on A624 which rises again before dropping to **Chapel-en-le Frith** (see page 60). Go under the first viaduct, turn left, and after the second

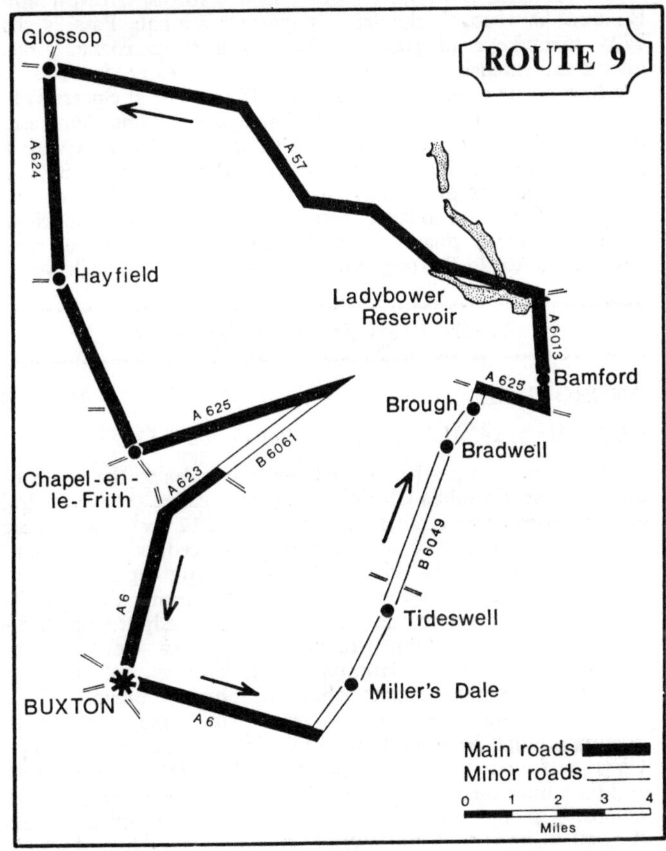

viaduct there is yet another curving round before us. When A6 is reached at Chapel-en-le-Frith turn left for Buxton. A6 can be followed through Barmoor Clough but for another scenic route turn left along A625 towards Sheffield, climbing yet again out of the softer scenery of the valley towards open moorland edged with gritstone walls. Ford Hall lies in the valley below, the home of William Bagshaw, the Apostle of the Peak. The low tower on the left skyline is the sole ventilating shaft of the Cowburn tunnel (1892). After five miles, as the road starts to drop towards Castleton below the shale layers of Mam Tor, turn right (B6061) for Sparrowpit and Buxton. (A road to the left signposted Winnats Pass is the 1725 turnpike road running through a steep rocky gorge, giving an extensive view towards Hope.) Nearer Sparrowpit the first of the cement works appear. Turn right at **Sparrowpit**, home of the first Peakland Methodist Society, along A623 and then left along A6. **Dove Holes** is an industrial village with a prehistoric circle, 200 yards round; only the ditch remains. The scene to the left gives the reason why the boundary of the National Park was pushed east, thus avoiding the workings of the Tunstead quarry, about a mile long. Soon the road descends towards Buxton, which it enters east of the town.

MAIN PLACES OF INTEREST

ASHBOURNE
Route 6

E.C. Wednesday, M.D. Saturday, Population 5,577

Ashbourne is a market town lying two miles to the south of the Peak. **St. Oswald's Church**, sometimes called the 'Cathedral of the Lower Peak', has a graceful spire 212 feet high, rising above a green sea of limes, yews and cedars. The south arcade of the medieval church has interesting capitals, one of them a carving of a green man — a face peering through the leaves. There are some fine monuments, especially the fifteenth-century figures of John Bradbourne and his wife and the alabaster tomb of Sir Humphrey Bradbourne and his wife surrounded by their sixteen children. The monuments of the Cokayne family provide contrast while the nineteenth-century pulpit is inset with Blue John stone. Sir Thomas Cokayne founded the **Grammar School** in 1585, a fine stone building now used for the boarders of the newly built school. Opposite is the red-brick building where Dr Johnson and Boswell visited Dr John Taylor. Johnson and Boswell stayed at the **Green Man** and **Black's Head** which still has an old sign stretching right across the road. Church Street continues its dignified appearance with **Pegg's almshouses** (1669) and **Owfield's almshouses** (1640). On Shrove Tuesday and Ash Wednesday anyone may join in the traditional game of football, played between goals 3 miles apart. Prince Charles Edward stayed at Ashbourne Hall on his march to Derby and again on his retreat. A road from the market place leads to the **Tissington Trail** walk, created from the old Ashbourne — Buxton railway line which closed in 1967. Car parks are at Alsop, Hartington, Tissington, Parsley Hay and Hurdlow.

BAKEWELL   Route 3

E.C. Thursday, M.D. Monday, Population 4,240

Bakewell is a pleasant market town well placed to serve as a base for tourists, anglers and sportsmen. It was probably a Saxon settlement and there is a Saxon **cross**, 8 feet high, in the churchyard and some carved Saxon stones are in the porch. The **church** has Norman remains at the west end but the present building is of fourteenth-century date with a rebuilt nave of 1852. In the south aisle is the alabaster tomb (1377) of Sir Godfrey Foljambe and his wife but the most famous monument is that to Sir John Manners and his wife, Dorothy Vernon, who is reputed to have eloped from Haddon Hall. Unfortunately the faces do not suggest such a romantic episode. Jane Austen stayed at the Georgian **Rutland Arms** and wrote parts of *Pride and Prejudice* there; Bakewell is probably Lambton and Chatsworth is Pemberley. The warm, brown stone of the houses contrasts with the white limestone of other villages. There is a seventeenth-century **meeting hall**, Georgian **almshouses** and a **bath house**, built in 1697 for the Duke of Rutland — all that remains of Bakewell's pretensions as a spa. The gardens behind this are an important feature. The **bridge** over the Wye is medieval; a little further upstream is a **packhorse bridge**. The town has given its name to one delicacy, Bakewell tart, which can still be bought.

BARLBOROUGH

E.C. Wednesday, Population 2,083

The **hall** was built in 1583 for Francis Roades and though it lacks the grandeur of Hardwick, its contemporary, is not without interest. The corner towers are crowned with battlements of semi-circles and squares. It is now a boys' preparatory school but is open to the public during the summer holidays.

BELPER Route 5

E.C. Wednesday, M.D. Saturday, Population 16,360

Edmund, Earl of Lancaster, had a hunting lodge here from which the town got its name *(Bel repère or Beau repaire)*. He also built a **chapel** nearby which still exists, a small thirteenth century building with lancet windows and a stone altar; the vestry has become a museum. Belper remained a small village until the 1770s when Jedediah Strutt joined with Richard Arkwright to build cotton mills. The township developed along the road towards Derby reaching out also to embrace the market-place of the old hamlet. The **North Mill**, rebuilt 1803-4 by William Strutt, survives, being now owned by English Sewing Ltd. It is iron-framed with cast-iron beams and columns. Gun embrasures can be seen in the bridge over the river, a precaution against Luddite attacks.

The Derwent has been called the cradle of the Industrial Revolution. Throughout its length can be seen the mills (or their remains) which established themselves on its bank utilising the water power. The water-wheels have almost all vanished but the weirs which held back the water survive in a variety of forms. Here, at Belper, is an upstream curved one. Some of the houses built by Strutt for his 3,000 employees are in existence; **Long Row,** near to the mill, and the **Clusters,** groups of four houses placed back to back. Other old houses have cast-iron window frames. Some small stone buildings are former nail-makers shops. The industry is first recorded in 1313 but died out in the mid-nineteenth century. The railway runs through the town in an impressive mile-long **cutting** lined with brick walls and crossed by ten bridges. When it was first made crowds came to admire the ingenuity of the engineers. **St. Peter's Church** is a good example of Victorian Gothic.

BOLSOVER

E.C. Wednesday, M.D. Friday, Population 11,770

The town itself is undistinguished but contains two buildings of great interest — the castle and the church. The first **castle** was medieval but in 1613 Sir Charles Cavendish, a son of Bess of Hardwick who inherited her passion for building, bought it and ordered John Smythson, son of Robert, to build a Jacobean version of a medieval keep. Sir Charles's son William, who became Earl (later Duke) of Newcastle, ordered Hartington Smythson, son of John, to build a riding school and a long range of buildings overlooking the valley. When Charles I and Henrietta Maria visited the castle in 1634 no effort was spared to entertain them, but the hatred of the

Parliamentarians meant that only ruins survived the Civil War. Repairs were made but centuries of decay have left merely a curiosity amongst architecture. The Department of the Environment is repairing the keep for subsidence has cracked the fabric. The view from the Chesterfield road looking up to this noble ruin is superb and wandering amongst the ruins brings reflections on the follies of a vanished age. Further reflections are inspired in the Cavendish Chapel in the **church** while gazing on the large monuments to Sir Charles (died 1617) and to the second Duke of Newcastle (died 1691). In the churchyard lie the bodies of the builders of Bolsover, John and Hartington Smythson.

BUXTON Routes 2, 7, 8 and 9

E.C. Wednesday, M.D. Saturday, Population 20,316

Paradoxically Buxton, though the capital of the Peak, is not in the Park. It was excluded because of its predominantly industrial surrounding, in particular the quarrying to the south. The *Aquae Arnemetiae* of the Romans, of which traces of lead-lined baths have been found, became a medieval centre for pilgrims who came to St. Anne's Well. Henry VIII closed the well and removed the relics, but the thermal springs still attracted visitors, in particular Mary, Queen of Scots, who had treatment for rheumatism and arthritis. The **Old Hall**, now an hotel, is on the site of the building where she stayed. The Dukes of Devonshire patronised the spring and the fifth Duke authorised John Carr to build the famous **Crescent**, a graceful curve 200 yards long, in 1784 (plate 10). It marked the beginning of the fashionable spa. Now the spa is closed but the **Devonshire Royal Hospital** still gives treatment. The waters are about 82°F and give relief to rheumatic complaints. They can be tasted at **St. Anne's well** in a small building opposite the Crescent. The **Pavilion** built in 1871, is used for conferences. Its gardens are open to the public and the river Wye flows through them, falling in cascades. The modern lower town, the main shopping centre, developed along the valley floor linked to the spa; the older upper town centres round the market place. Close by is **St. Anne's Chapel** built in 1625. There is a small museum with geological and archaeological remains. The town is an excellent centre from which to explore the Peak. Nearby are **Corbar Woods** created in the nineteenth century from old quarries. Two magnificent viewpoints are **Corbar Hill**, which looks down on the town and outward to Kinder Scout and Axe Edge, and **Solomon's Temple** on the slopes of Grin Low.

CHAPEL-EN-LE-FRITH   Route 9

E.C. Wednesday, M.D. Thursday, Population 6,460

Foresters founded a chapel here in 1225 — a chapel in the forest — but this has disappeared and the medieval **church,** dedicated to St. Thomas à Becket, was largely rebuilt in the eighteenth century. It is furnished with box-pews but in 1648 the interior must have been stripped, for 1500 Scots captured at the battle of Preston were crowded into the church and kept prisoner for sixteen days. At least 44 died in the church and others fell as they were released. The stocks remain in the market-place and there is a mounting block outside the Bull's Head. **Barmoor Clough** achieved fame for its ebbing and flowing well, whose level was always unpredictable, but now it is merely a marsh. **Combs Reservoir** on the A6 towards Whaley Bridge provides sailing for the weekend yachtsman. Its original use (1794-1800) was a feeder to the Peak Forest Canal.

CHESTERFIELD   Route 3

E.C. Wednesday, M.D. Monday & Saturday, Population 70,153

The outstanding feature of the town is the **Church of St. Mary and All Saints,** whose twisted spire is a result of the wood warping because of the sun's heat on the lead covering (plate 12). The twist is nearly 8 feet out of perpendicular and twice it has been near to destruction — once on a proposal to restore it, and again in 1961 from fire which burned out the north transept. Spire and church date from the fourteenth century. Only the font remains of the Norman church. The Foljambe chapel is filled with monuments including the effigy of Henry (died 1510) and his wife, the tomb chest of Sir Godfrey and the wall monument to Sir James. Few old buildings remain in the town which expanded rapidly when the railway arrived to open up the coalfield. The **Shambles** has a sixteenth-century building, the **Royal Oak,** and several Georgian buildings. Other street names are indicative of old trades — Saltergate, Knifesmithgate. The **Town Hall** dates to 1938, the shopping centre is modern and so is the **courthouse,** a rather striking building. George Stephenson stayed here while building the Midland Railway and liked the town so much that he bought **Tapton House,** just to the north. He is buried in the chancel of **Holy Trinity Church,** under the slab marked G.S. 1848. The library has a collection of Stephenson relics.

DERBY   Routes 4, 5 and 6

E.C. Wednesday, M.D. Friday & Saturday, Population 219,348

As the county town it is fitting that it should stand on the Derwent which flows through the county. The Romans had a fort at **Little Chester** *(Derventio)* but the town's real importance began in Saxon and Viking times when it was one of the five Midland 'burghs' or strongholds. In the Middle Ages it was an important market centre, especially in cloth, for King John gave it dyeing rights. The textile interest was exploited in 1777 when John and Thomas Lambe began the first successful silk mill which supplied silk thread to the framework knitters of Nottingham. The gates of the mill made by Robert Bakewell still survive and have been placed near the **Borough Library**. The growth of the silk industry brought prosperity to the town as can be seen from those Georgian houses which remain. A pottery works was begun with the object of making fine porcelain. In 1773 it was granted the right to mark a crown on it and so Crown Derby was created. Queen Victoria gave permission for 'Royal' to be added. A fine selection of the ware can be seen in the **Museum**. The original pottery is commemorated by a plaque in **Nottingham Road**. The pottery is now in **Osmaston Road** centred round what was the 1832 workhouse. The railway arrived in 1840 and the **Midland Station, Hotel** and adjacent buildings are basically those of 1841. The **locomotive workshops** were built in that year and the carriage and wagon works now cover 128 acres.

The impression today is that of a bustling city rather than one noted for its antiquities. The oldest building is perhaps the former **Bridge Chapel** by the river at the end of Bridge Gate, but it has been so much repaired that it is difficult to see the original work. Two old inns are the **Dolphin** of sixteenth-century date and the **Seven Stars** (1680), both much restored. The **Derwent Bridge** has medallions of four of Derby's most famous citizens, but not of Joseph Wright, known as Wright of Derby, whose paintings are world famous because of their treatment of light. A selection hangs in the **City Art Gallery**. The Gallery has recently been extended and contains pre-historic and Roman remains, examples of modern art, and features of the local and industrial scene including Rolls-Royce engines.

County Hall in St. Mary's Street is a fine classical building of 1660 with a simple, dignified interior but the new Council Offices completed in 1941 can only be considered as dull. **All Saints Church**, which became the Cathedral in 1927, retains its huge medieval Perpendicular tower 214 feet high but the rest of the church was replaced in 1723 by James Gibbs in uncompromising classical style (plate 14). The stern exterior, however, belies the interesting interior. The chancel screen is by Robert Bakewell, a fretwork of splendour. Monuments line the walls by Rysbrack, Roubiliac, Nollekens, Chantrey and Westmacott. A memorial in the south aisle is a reminder of **Prince Charles Edward Stuart's** stay here in 1745. A service was held in the church but at a fateful council meeting the decision was taken to retreat and the long road began which ended in tragedy on Culloden Moor. The largest monument is to Bess of Hardwick. Her effigy lies surrounded by thirteen smaller figures. For centuries the chapel was the burial place of the Cavendishes. More than 40 members of the family including some of the Dukes of Devonshire lie in the vault below.

St. Peter's is the only medieval church in the city, though much restored. Some of the original Norman arches survive. In the churchyard is the 1554 building which housed **Derby Grammar School** until the removal in 1863. **St. Werburgh's** was mainly rebuilt by Sir Arthur Blomfield in 1894 though he kept its older tower. Some of the furnishings are notable including the ironwork of Robert Bakewell. The Roman Catholic **St. Mary's** was built in Victorian-Gothic style in 1839 by Augustus Pugin; it is one of his best buildings. St. Alkmund's church stood opposite this and when pulled down in 1967 to make room for an underpass the original Saxon foundations were revealed. The church furnishings were re-used in a new church along **Kedleston Road**. They included the fourteenth-century font and carved Saxon stones. **St. John's** church has picturesque Gothic-style windows made of iron cast in the Britannia Foundry in 1827.

DOVEDALE Routes 1, 6 and 8

This is easily the most popular and probably the most beautiful of the dales. It is accessible only to walkers and though the path is surfaced from Thorpe to the **stepping stones** (plate 5), after that it can be rough and muddy. There is a car park near the entrance. From the top of **Thorpe Cloud** there is a good view of the Peak landscape, a high platform with gorges cut into it over the centuries by the rivers. Walking through the Dale we visit **Lover's Leap,** a spur of natural rock, and can see the **Twelve Apostles** and **Tissington Spires,** grey peaks of limestone emerging from the greenery. The dale bends so that there is a series of short vistas. There are even two caves, Dove Hole and **Reynard's Cave**, while the **Lion Rock** bears a distinct resemblance to that animal. **Thorpe** village stands on the edge of the valley, containing no notable houses, but attractive in itself with a church much restored, though retaining its Norman west tower, west door and font. **Ilam** village lies to the side of the dale. In the centre is the 'Eleanor cross' put up in memory of his wife by Jesse Watts-Russell, who built the Victorian-Gothic hall and village. The hall is now a youth hostel but the grounds (open to the public) give a good view of Thorpe Cloud and the countryside. The river Manifold rises here after flowing for four miles underground. The David Watts memorial by Sir Francis Chantrey, in the memorial chapel attached to the church, is striking. There are also two Saxon crosses, a Norman font, and a modern shrine to St. Bertram, who founded the original church about A.D. 700.

GLOSSOP
Route 9

E.C. Tuesday, M.D. Friday & Saturday, Population 24,147

In 1810 the area, then known as Howard's Town, had exactly two families, but by 1851 renamed Glossop contained a population of 28,625. Manufacturers were attracted to the site by the abundance of water power and workers flocked to the new mills. Many Catholic girls came to work for the Catholic firms. The town is an interesting example of a nineteenth-century industrial community. The complex of **Wren's Nest mill** was begun in 1815 and the paper mills of Thomas Ibbotson date from 1837. The **market hall** dates from 1834 and the railway builders added to the dramatic effect with a splendid viaduct 120 feet high stretching across the Dinting valley, originally of sixteen arches, each of 125-foot span. Unfortunately they have had to be reinforced. To the north-east is **Old Glossop**, a community of older houses, one dated to 1638. The **parish church** was rebuilt in this century. William Bagshaw, the Apostle of the Peak, was rector in the old church until he was ejected after the Act of Uniformity (1662) because of his refusal to accept the Prayer Book. On a hill to the west is a Roman Catholic chapel (1836) and between church and chapel lies **Glossop Hall**, built in the last century for Lord Howard de Glossop, in the style of a French *château*. Now this house is a school and the grounds are a public park. The National Park swings in a great circle round Glossop which regards itself as a northern gateway to the Peak. To the north of the Dinting Valley lies **Melandra Castle**, the most northerly of the Roman forts in Derbyshire. **Doctor's Gate**, a Roman road, may be traversed on foot from Old Glossop southwards across the moors. Northwest is **Dinting Railway Centre** where several restored steam engines are preserved.

HADDON HALL

The hall is two miles south-east of Bakewell on A6. Haddon is one of the finest medieval houses in England. It was built about 1370 on the site of an earlier house, part of which still survives. The house was the home of the Vernons until 1567 when it passed to Sir George's daughter who had married Sir John Manners. His descendants, as Dukes of Rutland, own the house today. In 1912 the ninth Duke decided to have the house restored and it is now in a fine state of preservation. Its romantic outlook reflects the romantic story of the elopement of Dorothy Vernon and John Manners in 1563. The wall paintings in the chapel date from the fifteenth century, the kitchens and great hall from 1370. The Tudor Vernons added the other rooms including the State Bedroom and the Long Gallery. The seventeenth-century terraced gardens are best seen in summer when the roses are out. These look down on the packhorse bridge where John Manners waited for his beloved.

HARDWICK HALL

This vast house was the last one built by Bess of Hardwick, who married firstly Robert Barlow, secondly Sir William Cavendish, thirdly Sir William St. Loe, and lastly George Talbot, sixth Earl of Shrewsbury, all of whom left her immense fortunes with which to indulge her building whims. Legend said that she believed she would not die while building was in progress. Hard frost stopped work in 1607 and she did die at the age of 87. Hardwick was in the hands of the Dukes of Devonshire until 1957 when the house was taken in settlement of death duties and was handed over to the National Trust. Robert Smythson built the house (1590-97) as a compact and symmetrical block unlike the rambling houses of earlier dates. The Drawing Room, High Great Chamber and Long Gallery are filled with fine furnishings, much of it original to the house. The tapestries are splendid; those in the High Great Chamber and the Long Gallery were purchased before the house was built and the rooms were designed round them. Each room has its place in the overall magnificence. The exterior lives up to the tag 'more glass than wall' while the initials ES (Elizabeth of Shrewsbury) dominate the house as she herself must have done during her lifetime.

MANIFOLD VALLEY   Routes 1, 6 and 8

Like Dovedale this is accessible only to the walker for the first four miles from Ilam although the path runs not in the dale but high above it.   In the northern part from above **Weag's Bridge** the path follows the line of the light railway closed in 1934. **Beeston Tor** rises above the valley, whose side contains several caves, the most famous being **Thor's Cave.** Motorists can cross the valley, up and down the steep hills, from Butterton to Wetton and from Grindon to Alstonefield, or run along a narrow track from Wetton to Hulme End.

MATLOCK   Routes 3 and 5

E.C. Thursday, M.D. Tuesday & Saturday, Population 19,575

This town is also excluded from the National Park but its position is somewhat similar to Buxton for it is the eastern gateway to the Peak. The Matlocks is the collective name for Matlock Bank, Matlock Town, Matlock Bridge, Matlock Bath and Matlock Dale strung out along the Derwent Valley. It was probably a lead-mining centre in Roman times but its modern history begins in 1698 when a bath-house was erected for visitors to take the waters. In the eighteenth century it was a fashionable spa and in 1815 a new road was extended through the valley from Belper to Cromford. When the gentry departed, the coming of the railway in 1849 ensured the arrival of the middle classes. Today the town is busy with day visitors. At **Matlock Bath** the water issuing from the limestone at a temperature of 68°F. feeds a fishpond by the **Pavilion,** while the pump room allows a taste of the thermal water. It also wells up in the **Aquarium** with its fresh water and tropical fish. Nearby is the **Petrifying Well,** where there are always objects waiting to be turned to stone. **Matlock Bank** rises in tiers above the valley, each tier being reached by a steep street. There is a splendid view of the town from the **Victoria Tower.** John Smedley built his hydro here in 1853 and followed it with **Riber Castle,** a private residence for himself. The grounds are now a fauna reserve and wild life park which breeds species of British birds and mammals (open to the public). The **hydro,** the east wing neo-classical, the west Victorian-Gothic, is now used by Derbyshire County Council. Many of the other large buildings in the town were originally hydros. **All Saints Church** has stained glass by Morris. **Matlock Bridge** is the shopping centre grouped round the fifteenth-century bridge. **Hall Leys** gardens run along the bank of the Derwent and a path leads from them up to Pic Tor and then on to High Tor. **Matlock Town** is the oldest part, sited high above the valley, centred on the green and the church. **St. Giles's,** rebuilt in the nineteenth century, retains its medieval tower and has a glass case containing maiden garlands or crants. On the west wall is the black marble memorial of Adam Woolley who died aged 100 in 1657 and his wife Grace, who died aged 110 in 1669. Matlock is unfortunately commercially exploited but the grandeur of the natural scenery extends to the **Heights of Abraham** and **High Tor,** and the **Great Rutland, Cumberland** and **Masson Caverns.**

NEW MILLS

E.C. Wednesday, M.D. Friday & Saturday, Population 8,880

The name derives from the new corn mills built here about 1500 for Henry VII. A town grew up lying on the western edge of the county with moorland to north and south and shadowed on the east by Kinder Scout. Some seventeenth and eighteenth-century cottages remain and the **Bull's Head** is Georgian, but the town is still dominated by the mills of the Industrial Revolution, strung out along the valleys. The **Town Hall** stands above the valley and the railway viaduct strides across it, rising 100 feet above the Goyt.

TIDESWELL
Routes 2 and 9

E.C. Tuesday, Population 1,829

This is a small limestone-built town which grew up round industry and agriculture. It is still a market centre but the lead-mining and stone-quarrying have ceased and the textile works are closed. The industrial workers have been replaced by visitors who admire the vast fourteenth-century **church** — the 'Cathedral of the Peak'. There are many monuments including a brass to Bishop Pursglove (died 1579) and the table tomb of Sir Sampson Meverill, Constable of England under Henry VI. By long custom the marriage register is signed on this tomb. The **George,** by the side of the church, is a pleasant Georgian inn. From Tideswell a road leads to **Wheston** where a remarkable fourteenth-century wayside cross survives — one side portrays the Crucifixion, the other the Nativity.

WIRKSWORTH
Route 5

Population 5,040

For centuries Wirksworth has been the centre of the lead-mining industry. Lead was exploited by the Romans and in medieval times the Barmoot Court emerged to decide claims relating to lead-mining. It still meets in the **Moot Hall** (1814), which houses the standard measuring dish of 1513 and has the symbols of Justice carved above the door. Other nineteenth-century buildings are the **Grammar School** (first founded in 1584) and the **Compleat Angler.** The **Red Lion** is Georgian while the oldest houses are probably **Babington House** (1588) and **Gell's Almshouses** (1584). **St. Mary's Church** is basically thirteenth-century with a fourteenth-century tower, but restored by Sir George Gilbert Scott in 1876. In the north aisle is a carved Saxon stone showing scenes from the Gospels—a rare survival. There are fine groups of sixteenth-century monuments relating to the Blackwalls and the Gells. **Providence Mill,** first recorded in 1823, continues to weave strips of fabric, The houses nearby date from the same time. **Willowbath Mill** is a low stone building on a main branch of the Ecclesbourne, mentioned in 1816; it produces red tape for tying up documents. **Haarlem Mill** was made famous by George Eliot's Adam Bede whose cottage is opposite. Wirksworth claims to be 'Snowfield' and in the churchyard under the copper beech lies Elizabeth Evans, the 'Diana Morris' of the novel. The **Methodist chapel** where she preached still stands.

PHOTOGRAPHS

Photographs are acknowledged as follows: Joan P. Alcock, plates 4, 10, 16, 18; R. D. Barrett-Lennard, plate 8; Robert D. Bristow, plates 3, 11, 12, 14, 15, 19, 20, 21; G. H. Haines, plates 9, 13, 17; G. J. Hollister-Short, plate 2; Mrs. E. Preston, plates 1, 5, 6, 7.

INDEX OF PLACES

Printed by C. I. Thomas & Sons (Haverfordwest) Ltd.
Merlin's Bridge, Haverfordwest, Pembrokeshire